To Ride the Heights

LINDA FOUST GRAJEWSKI

"The Sovereign LORD is my strength;
he makes my feet like the feet of a deer,
he enables me to tread on the heights."

HABAKKUK 3:19

Preface

Growing up on a cattle farm had a lot of advantages. One such advantage was teaching me to listen to God by listening to His creation. Many times on a summer evening, I would sit on the front porch swing and listen to the whip-poor-wills and bobwhites as they called to each other. It was a time to de-stress and process the events of the day, something almost lost in our modern society of multi-tasking, instant electronic communication, and air conditioning.

TWILIGHT

In the softening twilight,
While the earth prepares for rest.
Comes the time I sit and think.
Of those that I love best.
Peace and contentment overcome me at this time,
And I feel as if this moment were planned for all mankind.
To pause and meditate,
To time pay no mind,
With the world be at ease,
And as one with God.

If you but take this moment,
And use it as I've said.
You'll find that of tomorrow,
You've lost your fear and dread.

"For the creation waits in eager expectation for
the children of God to be revealed."
ROMANS 8:19

In those days, the school bus would let my brother and I off about a half mile from our home. We would then walk the old dirt road that was bounded by our grandfather's pastures on one side, and woods on the other. I enjoyed these slow walks of transition from school to home, but especially in the spring.

OLD DIRT ROAD

To walk along an old dirt road,
Quit early in the Spring.
To see the hidden beauty,
Around each curve that wings.
To walk in calm serenity,
With God myself and man.
This is what I ask from life,
I'll give back all I can.

"He has shown you, O mortal, what is good.
And what does the Lord require of you?
*To act justly and to love mercy and to **walk humbly** with your God."*
MICAH 6:8

Introduction

When an artist paints a picture, it is always the dark that reveals the depth and beauty of the subject. And so it is with our lives. I am an adult child of an alcoholic parent. My father battled that illness until it took his life drinking and driving. Alcoholism is a weird disease in that it also infects the family and friends surrounding the individual. We hid my father's drinking for many years. It helped in that he was a binge drinker and not daily drinker until his later years when it could no longer be denied and hidden. In many ways, my father was good and loving, a capable businessman, and respected in our community. But, as he became more ill, so did I. I developed very unhealthy ways of dealing or not dealing with relationships. I became a perfectionist, an over-achiever, a people pleaser and a raging co-dependent.

I am sharing this with you because God tells us:

"They will tell of the glory of your kingdom and speak of your might,
so that all men may know of your mighty acts and
the glorious splendor of your kingdom."
PSALM 134:11–12

This is a story of how God helped me to heal and how He tore down my "high places of sacrifice" and enabled me to ride the heights with Him.

Eighty percent or more of the children of alcoholics/addicts themselves become alcoholics/addicts. The only reason I am not is because at the age of thirteen, I surrendered my life, as best I knew how, to Jesus Christ. I would like to say that I never made a mistake and that life was easy and comfortable after that, but it would not be true. I had a lot of growing, healing, and learning to do, but I did not have to do it alone.

My story is not about one ordinary life, but what ONE EXTRAORDINARY God did with that life. Thanks for coming along on my journey. As I write my story, I am praying for you, dear reader, that God will use it to encourage, uplift, and, yes, challenge you to tear down your "high places of sacrifice" so you, too, can ride the heights with Him.

"They have built the high places of Baal to burn their children in the fire as offerings to Baal—something I did not command or mention, nor did it enter my mind."
JEREMIAH 19:5

High Places of Sacrifice

What does this mean for us today? High places of sacrifice are many and varied, but the one common factor is that they are built by us and not by God. God says that not only did He not tell us to build them, He didn't even think about it. God also warns us that if we do not tear them down, He will. I believe one reason He speaks so strongly to us on this issue is because our children suffer and are sacrificed upon these altars of our pride and selfishness. Some high places are generational and have become real strongholds that take a lot of prayer and hard work to tear down. Throughout this book, I will share mine and how God dealt with them. One of them for me and my family was alcohol.

*"I will destroy your **high places**…"*
LEVITICUS 26:30

As a young adult, I did drink alcoholic beverages socially. But, later when I married and was teaching middle school and high school teens, God dealt with me on this issue. Almost every one of my students would ask me, "Coach, do you drink"? I became very convicted about my influence on them. I went to the Word of God for wisdom and advice and found it:

"Therefore let us stop passing judgment on one another. Instead, make up your Mind not to put any stumbling block or obstacle in your brother's way. It is better not to eat meat or drink wine or to do anything else that will cause your brother to fall."
ROMANS 14:13

"Be careful, however, that the exercise of your freedom does not become a stumbling block to the weak."
1 CORINTHIANS 8:9

So this "high place of sacrifice" was torn down in my life by God's Word. But, there were still many more that God would deal with through the years.

Beginnings

At the age of twenty-three, I was teaching college. I was too young and foolish to realize the challenges of that situation. Being very immature in my faith and needing many high places torn down, I struggled through those years. But, it was here that I met my husband. Neither of us was living life God's way when we met. After we married, we both rededicated our lives and our home to Him. In fact, it was during the fourth year of our marriage that God tore down the high place of alcohol in both our lives.

My husband was a senior at the college where I was teaching. He loves telling people he married his teacher but that is not exactly true, as he never had me for a class. But, when he graduated, the college I was teaching at closed, and we were both unemployed and the unemployment rate in Alabama was almost twelve percent at that time.

A friend of mine and her husband were living in a suburb of Houston, Texas, and she invited us to come there and look for employment. We did and through a series of meetings and connections, both of us ended up finding jobs within three days in the town of Temple, Texas.

I did not understand it at the time, but God was going to do in my life what I was not capable of. He was going to tear down my high places of sacrifice and replace them with His heights of obedience and blessing. But most of the time, I would not enjoy the process.

"I will destroy your high places."
EZEKIEL 6:3

Birth

Never did I expect to have the overwhelming experience of love that I did with the birth of my first son. I thought I knew love with my husband and parents but this feeling was new and different…it was selfless. I knew that I would do anything and everything for that tiny bit of humanity in my arms. Then when I was pregnant with my second son, I was so worried that I could not possibly love another child as much as the first. Yet, again when that tiny person was placed in my arms, the overwhelming power of love came. I think this is the closest we can possibly come to understanding the love of God for us. Through this, God began to tear down another "high place of sacrifice" in my life—that of division. I learned that the mathematical equation with love is "addition and multiplication."

"Flesh gives birth to flesh, but the Spirit gives birth to spirit."
JOHN 3:6

*"He chose to give us birth through the word of truth,
that we might be a kind of firstfruits of all he created."*
JAMES 1:18

*"Praise be to the God and Father of our Lord Jesus Christ!
In his great mercy he has given us new birth into a living hope
through the resurrection of Jesus Christ from the dead…"*
1 PETER 1:3

Birth—the very word reminds us of the pains of labor that make it possible. Birth also implies newness, immaturity, and an expectation of growth. But just as my children had to learn and grow, so did I. The Bible refers to this as being babes in Christ. It is not enough to just be "born again," we must seek to grow up in Him.

*"Like newborn babies, crave pure spiritual milk, so that by it you may grow
up in your salvation…"*
1 PETER 2:2

Seasons

Many people refer to the "seasons" of their life as stages or age; the childhood, adult, and senior years. But for me, these were and are continuous throughout my life. We think that our growth happens in the times of spring or summer, not in the times of drought or winter, but that is not exactly true. During the periods in my life when my spiritual life seemed dry, and I could not hear the voice of God or feel His presence, when there were difficulties and the winds of winter raged around me, I would question God, sometimes His very existence. I did not realize then but those times were to make me more fruitful and productive in my life. They removed the "dead branches" and things that hindered my walk with Him and others. Also, during the dry times is when a tree's roots must go deep into the earth seeking moisture. So it is with our lives. It is these times that force us to reach and grow into the deep things of the Spirit of God.

"And the remnant that is escaped of the house
of Judah shall again take root downward,
and bear fruit upward…"
ISAIAH 37:31

"Every branch in me that beareth not fruit he taketh away: and every branch that beareth fruit, he purgeth it, that it may bring forth more fruit."
JOHN 15:2

It is also these times that teach us not to rely on our own ability and capability but on Him. For those of us in bondage to the high place of perfectionism and over-achievement, this sometimes is a continuous life-long lesson.

"Abide in me, and I in you. As the branch cannot bear fruit of itself, except it abide in the vine; no more can ye, except ye abide in me."
JOHN 15:4

Depression

The first time I faced this demon was my sophomore year in college. Being in bondage to perfectionism, I dared not let anyone know. Also, in those days, most people did not talk about this. It was considered a "spiritual" issue by most in the church and meant that you were sinning and needed to repent, read your Bible, and pray. This attitude only added to my belief of not being enough. Many times the root cause of depression is physiological and not spiritual or psychological. I was fortunate in that my depression was not debilitating as some face, but it did make everything harder, and though it did not rob me of my life, it did rob me of much joy during those periods.

Can depression be a tool in the hand of God? Absolutely YES! Many of the prophets and spiritual leaders throughout history have struggled with this. However, an example of how this is still misunderstood within Christian circles is that when I did a topical search on depression from a biblical resource, there was nothing available. Most ministers do not understand mental illness and are themselves fearful of dealing with it. Yet statistics say that one-fourth of our population is struggling with a mental disorder at any given time. This is a "high place of sacrifice" that a huge number within the church are dealing with and many do so in isolation, often feeling abandoned by their church and God.

As I have studied the lives of others in the Bible, and stories through the centuries, I have found that many have battled this affliction and have been victorious over it.

Now, LORD, take away my life, for it is better for me to die than to live.
JONAH 4:3

…while he himself went a day's journey into the wilderness. He came to a broom bush, sat down under it and prayed that he might die. "I have had enough, LORD," he said. "Take my life; I am no better than my ancestors."
1 KINGS 19:4

Should good be repaid with evil? Yet they have dug a pit for me…
JEREMIAH 18:20

Surely it was for my benefit that I suffered such anguish. In your love you kept me from the pit of destruction; you have put all my sins behind your back.
ISAIAH 38:17

Home

I loved my home community and people. My family had lived there for more than six generations and I never wanted to live anywhere else. But God had a different plan for my life. This one for me was a really difficult and long lesson. God took me to Texas dragging my heels all the way. In spite of my reluctance, Temple, Texas, where the boys were born, was very good to us. We prospered and we made wonderful friends there. However, when our oldest was two years old and the baby two months old, my husband decided to make a career change. That was the beginning of five moves over the next two years. My "high places" just do not come down easy. I struggle with a very strong self-will. God was teaching me through this that "HOME is where the Lord is." I did not realize that I had made an idol of my home community and it had a place in my heart before God. Through this, God showed me that wherever I was, He was there first, and if He was there, I was home with Him. This was before the book, *The Prayer of Jabez* was published, so I did not know that God Himself was doing this in my life.

God so wanted to enlarge my territory but I was such a reluctant Christ follower in those days. Self was still on the throne and battling for its own way. The other problem was the almost constant voice of the enemy as he whispered in my ear, "you are not enough, not good enough, smart enough...."

My next high place was about to be pulled down. I would learn that I am not enough but that was to be replaced by the "Great I Am."

Jabez cried out to the God of Israel,
"Oh, that you would bless me and enlarge my territory!
Let your hand be with me, and keep me from harm
so that I might not cause pain."
And God granted his request...
1 CHRONICLES 4:10

I Am

The struggle to replace the "I" in our lives with the "Great I Am" is often the most difficult hurdle we will face. It was during these early years that I discovered a book and program called "The Search for Significance" by Dr. Robert McGee. After reading and working through this in a group study, I really begin to understand the root of my high places—Satan's lies. The challenging and painful process of replacing Satan's lies with God's truth had begun.

The first of these lies—I must meet certain standards to feel good about myself—is also centered in a fear of failure. Here was the root cause of my perfectionism. But no longer denying something does not mean that it goes away immediately. I have worked on this and allowed the "Great I Am" to do so also, and have made much progress over the years. Our society and culture is in bondage to these lies also.

There is a line from an old hymn, "just as I am." That is how we come to Him and how we please Him. He is our Creator and to do anything else is to devalue who He created you to be. The only way to replace the "I" with the "Great I Am" is to come to Him. This is the only sure way not to fail.

God said to Moses, "I AM WHO I AM.
This is what you are to say to the Israelites: 'I AM has sent me to you.'"
EXODUS 3:14

This is love: not that we loved God,
but that he loved us and sent his Son as an atoning sacrifice for our sins.
1 JOHN 4:10

Follow God's example, therefore, as dearly loved children...
EPHESIANS 5:1

$\mathcal{D}$riven

That is the word that best describes how I functioned as a volleyball coach but the one in the driver's seat wasn't God. I was coaching at the smallest college in the state but was blessed with an incredibly talented and diverse group of young women. We had such a high ranking season that even though we did not win our state, we were given a bid to go to Nationals. Because of this precious team, I was voted Jr. College Volleyball Coach of the Year. One year I even served as the Athletic Director, the only female one in the state, and definitely the youngest also. But nothing was enough for me. I needed more.

When the college closed and we moved to Texas, I ended up coaching high school again. My team lost Regions to the same team two years in a row and by only one point each time. But we did win a lot of tournament trophies during the season. God was so gracious to allow me to be a part of these girls' lives and for us to have the successful seasons that we did.

I did not intend to be a coach but women's sports were just coming into popularity and there were not enough coaches. So when I graduated, though ill prepared, I found that to have a job, I had to coach. This definitely did not fit into my career plans. I wanted to get my PhD and be a college professor. I thought that being called "Doctor" would bring me the esteem I so desired. But my plan and God's plan collided and the result wasn't pretty at first.

Many are the plans in a person's heart,
but it is the LORD's purpose that prevails.
PROVERBS 19:21

"But they will reply, 'It's no use. We will continue with our own plans; we
will all follow the stubbornness of our evil hearts.'"
JEREMIAH 18:12

Made New

My Father was diagnosed with lung cancer in the fall of 1980. I was teaching at Belton ISD in Belton, Texas. My principal graciously allowed me to stay in the teacher's lounge by the phone during his surgery. As I waited for the call, I prayed and asked God to please give us ten more years. I don't really know how I came up with that number, it just came to me. I asked Him to allow our family to heal and enjoy each other more. My dad had the infected lung removed and was given a good prognosis for recovery.

Amazing things happened for our family over the next several years. My dad recovered but was handicapped, having only one lung was a limitation, but he was with us. It was during these years the boys were born, our moves started, and God started working on my healing. The incredible thing was the more I healed, the better all the relationships around me were.

My parents were the best grandparents and were constantly coming to Texas to spend time with us. Much joy was shared during those years.
The Christmas of 1989, we decided to go home for the Holidays. But when we arrived my dad was drunk. This was the first time the boys had seen him like this and it was devastating after an almost thirteen-hour drive to have to deal with someone in his condition. But something happened in him and he began to sober up. He did not want the boys to

see him that way either. By Christmas Eve, things were better and we all had a good though tempered evening at my grandfather's home. As much as I tried, there was still a deep sadness because within myself I always thought if my dad loved me enough, he would not do this. I did not understand the disease of alcoholism. That Christmas morning, we awoke to the first white Christmas we had ever had. Snow had not even been predicted. I heard God whisper in my spirit, "behold I make ALL things new again." It ended up being the most wonderful Christmas Day we had ever had.

And he that sat upon the throne said, Behold, I make all things new.
And he said unto me, Write: for these words are true and faithful.
REVELATION 21:5

True and Faithful

I write this praying for the wisdom of the Holy Spirit to come and use my hand to record His truth, for I recognize that some will not understand or believe. That is between them and God. My job is to submit to His leading in loving obedience.

In August of 1990, the boys and I visited my parents on their farm for a couple of weeks. It was the best time any of us could remember. My dad and I would sit on the front porch talking, laughing, and watching the boys play. Then they took us home to Texas.

Usually my parents would wake up about 2 or 3 in the morning and quietly sneak out of the house before any of us were awake. So our habit was to say our good-byes the evening before. I had kissed my dad, told him that I loved him, and thanked him for such a wonderful trip. Then my parents went on to bed. When I finally was ready for bed myself, I had to pass their room before coming to mine. As I did so, it was as if a hand grabbed my shoulder to stop me and a voice said, "Go and kiss your Father. You are not going to have him much longer." As this had never happened to me before, I kind of shrugged it off, but turned to my parents' room and looking at his aged and weary face, thought that voice was from me. But it came a second time prompting me to go and kiss him again and repeat my love and thanks, which I did. One week later I received the call from my mother that we had always feared. Dad had been killed in a single vehicle accident while drinking and driving. Words cannot express how grateful we were that he took no one else with him, and that in His mercy, God had taken him instantly without a mark on his earthly body.

My Father died on August 27, 1990, almost exactly ten years from his cancer surgery.

God again set a certain day, calling it "Today." This he did when a long time later he spoke through David, as in the passage already quoted: "Today, if you hear his voice, do not harden your hearts."
HEBREWS 4:7

...for he is our God and we are the people of his pasture, the flock under his care. Today, if only you would hear his voice...
PSALM 95:7

Acceptance

The second of Satan's lies that I had to overcome in my life was that I must be accepted by others in order to feel good about myself. This was the root of another high place I struggled with, that of being a "people pleaser."

In November, after my Father passed away, my husband received a promotion, and transfer. We were moving again but this time out of Texas to the New Orleans area. We thought this was to be a short-term move but that became twelve years for me and fifteen years for my husband. I was to struggle here as nowhere else in my life. I am reminded of how a caterpillar grows inside a cocoon and when he is fully formed must struggle to break out of that cocoon. Though he is a fully formed butterfly at this stage, if someone comes and opens that cocoon for him, he will not be able to fly. It is the struggle that makes his wings strong. I now know that is one of the reasons God left me so long in an area where I just seemed so out of place. Also, it was here that I learned some of my greatest lessons from Him.

I brought my horse from the farm to live in Louisiana with us. Without my father there to care for her, she was a burden my mom did not need. My mother had always been afraid of horses, while my father and I loved them passionately. I boarded her at a stable near our home and went to feed and ride her daily. It was here also that I fulfilled a lifelong dream of taking riding lessons in dressage and jumping. I was beginning to learn that when we lay down our plans and pick up God's, He has some wonderful surprises hidden within them.

After dealing with hurricanes and street flooding for a year and a half, we made the decision to move a few miles north to higher ground. There we would also be able to have a few acres and keep my horse on our own property. Our oldest would be entering fifth grade and the youngest third grade when we moved to Mississippi. I was excited and almost felt like I was coming home to raise my boys in this small town. I desperately wanted to fit in and be accepted by the people there.

I had not yet learned that the surest way to fail at anything was to try and please everybody.

Am I now trying to win the approval of human beings,
or of God? Or am I trying to please people?
If I were still trying to please people,
I would not be a servant of Christ.
GALATIANS 1:10

Strangers

I had surrendered my desire to have a PhD but through all of that passion into being "Super Mom" and "Super Christian." I had a hard time learning that not every good thing is from God and not every good thing from God is for me. If I was staying home and did not have a title to share whenever someone asked me what I did, then I would just tell them how much I did. I signed up to be a Home Room Mother for both boys and an officer in the PTA, as well as numerous other church and community activities. It is just exhausting for me to even think about how much I thought I had to do in order to please everyone and, oh yes, God, too. But that first year in Mississippi, I met a very special friend. She and I shared the Home Room Mother duties for the third grade class. I am so blessed because she was patient and gracious with me through the years and is still a friend today. We loved to meet once in a while for breakfast and one such morning, an extraordinary thing happened.

As we sat eating breakfast, my view was of the exit and access ramps of the interstate. I saw a car stop and let out what I thought was a slender young girl with long, blonde hair. It was a cold morning, at least by south Mississippi standards. I said to my friend, "Oh no, look at that young girl." She turned and looked and then both of us left the restaurant and went out to get her. We discovered she was not a young girl but a woman around our age, and her face showed the bruises and marks of a recent beating. As the events unfolded, we were able to get her a motel room for the weekend, and this was Friday. But the rules were she would have to be willing to look for a job on Monday or leave.

She told me that she did not want to leave her room. So my youngest son and I visited her several times over the weekend, carrying her food. Every time we came, she would have her Bible open and artwork out. As her story unfolded, she said that she was a Christian and that God was preparing her to be used to help other believers during the End Times. When I went by on Monday before dropping the boys off for school, she was gone and no one had seen her leave. Was she just some poor mentally ill woman or something more? I do not know. But I am glad that I did not miss this God appointment because I was keeping myself so busy with my own errands.

Do not forget to show hospitality to strangers,
for by so doing some people have shown hospitality
to angels without knowing it.
HEBREWS 13:2

Appointments

When we moved to Mississippi, I decided to look into going back into teaching and checked with the local officials. I found out that with a Masters, teaching certifications from three different states, and nine years of experience, that I would still have to go back and be recertified as a first-year teacher. I sought advice from several different people and found out at that time, Mississippi had a very complicated and lengthy certification program. One person said she could have gotten her Masters with all the extra work required. Mississippi did away with that program after a few years, but not before I made the decision to try my hand at real estate.

My Aunt had been an agent for more than twenty years and with all of our moves and my real estate experiences, I thought this would be a good match for me. I don't remember how much I consulted God about this, however. But during the six years that I worked as an Agent, I would learn to pray and consult Him about everything. I did seek accountability from several of my friends on this endeavor, and I almost wore them out with my calls of whining, complaining, and asking for advice.

In spite of my shortcomings, God blessed my work and helped provide much needed finances during the expensive high school years for the boys. He also allowed me to be a part of blessing others with new homes and the jobs those new constructions created as I worked for local contractors. But after I had been in the business not quite three years, I had an accident that would greatly change the direction of my life.

Growing up on a farm, I was taught to drive tractors and learned how to drive a vehicle by driving my dad's ton cattle truck. So it was nothing to me to try and drive a Bobcat, which is a smaller type of heavy earth moving equipment. We had leased this in order to form the foundation for a new barn we were having built. But they are really made for larger men to drive. I did well for a while but was too short to see clearly and hit a small stump. This set the Bobcat to rocking and slipped me down in the seat. Even though I had a seatbelt on, it did not keep me tight enough and my foot was thrown outside and crushed. I was able to turn off the machine and crawl to the house and dial 911. As the accident was happening, I heard that voice again. This time it said, "You have to go through this but everything will be all right." This would prove to be one of the defining moments of my life.

> *Listen! The LORD is calling to the city—*
> *and to fear your name is wisdom—*
> *"Heed the rod and the One who appointed it."*
> MICAH 6:9

Opinions

I was taken to the hospital not in our town but a larger one because of the severity of my injury where the surgeon did an emergency operation. I would go back to him as my attending physician and be released several months later. But at my release, he did not x-ray my foot but said if you have any problems come back. I even asked if he was going to x-ray my foot before he released me and he said no.

I did have problems but something within me said I needed to get another opinion, so I called my primary care doctor and asked him who he would send his wife to. To make a long story short, the new doctor looked at my foot said something is not right and immediately x-rayed it. It was almost identical to the original x-rays that I had brought in. It was still broken and displaced. The bones were not even touching. This ended up causing me to have two more surgeries and being in a wheelchair or on crutches for a total of a year and a half. But because of this, my oldest son was saved from being handicapped or disabled.

When my oldest was in the 8th grade, the school did a scoliosis screening and sent home a message that he needed to be checked by a doctor. This was prior to my accident. The orthopedic doctor we were referred to was the one who would later miss the diagnosis and proper treatment for my injured foot. This doctor just did a visual, no x-ray, of my son's back and said, "This boy just needs to exercise." I had nagging doubts but in my busyness, just ignored them. But after this doctor missed something as obvious as my broken foot, I decided to have my son checked by another doctor.

I again called our primary care doctor and asked for a referral, telling him the entire story. He referred us to a specialist on the Mississippi coast. The minute I walked into this precious man's office, I was at peace. He was an incredibly caring and gifted physician. I believe he knew immediately what was wrong with my son but spoke directly to him and said he needed an x-ray. The x-ray revealed that a section of my son's spine, about 4 discs, was compressed toward the inside, resulting in the rounding of his back at the lower part of his shoulder blades. The doctor said this was commonly called, "Sherman's Round back." The miracle, he said, was at the age of seventeen, a male's spine fuses and nothing could be done. My son was fifteen and a half. We had a small window of opportunity. He would wear a full body brace twenty-three of twenty-four hours a day for the next year. Within three months, he grew two inches as the pressure was removed from his growth plates. He had a great attitude through this ordeal and used humor as much as possible to deflect negative comments. God had to do something drastic to get my attention, but my son now has a normal back.

"For I know the plans I have for you," declares the LORD,
"plans to prosper you and not to harm you,
plans to give you hope and a future."
JEREMIAH 29:11

Psychic Hot Line

During that year and a half, God also did a work within me deepening my prayer life. After my first surgery, I was feeling sorry for myself one day and sitting on my front porch praying or rather whining to Him about how I could not do all the things for Him that I had been doing. Immediately after I said Amen, the phone rang. I picked it up and said hello. There was a hesitation on the other end and then a woman's voice said, "Is this the psychic hot line?" I laughed, thinking one of my friends was teasing me, and said, "No, but I know the only true psychic there is. His name is Jesus. Can I tell you about Him?" It was not a joke. This woman was calling in desperate need of help from another state hundreds of miles away. We laughed and talked about God's love for us to connect in this unusual way.

We had several phone conversations over the next few weeks as I mentored her to start attending a local church and Bible study group sharing what God had done for her. She then was able to find a job and start working about the time I also went back to work on crutches. From this, I slowly started learning to let go of my plans and look for the God appointments in my life, for this certainly was one, and one I would have missed if God had not forced me to be still.

The drugs that I was given during surgery had a very negative effect on me. After each surgery I felt as if I were in the bottom of a well and could not climb out. It did not go away over the months in between, but with each subsequent surgery was made worse. I even found myself zoning out at times and not being able to transfer numbers from my checkbook to my ledger. I had prided myself on my quick mind, especially with numbers, and even began having small panic attacks. I did not share this with very many people but struggled on in my pride. Because of the instability this caused me emotionally, I changed real estate companies twice during this and finally quit all together.

One day my Pastor was teasing me and said, "Now, Linda, some people are wondering why it is taking so long for your foot to heal. You just need to have faith." I laughed and told him, "No, Pastor. It is taking so long because you have not laid hands on it and prayed." I think not only was God teaching me but others around me.

"The LORD will fight for you; you need only to be still."
EXODUS 14:14

Horses

When I was five, my grandfather bought us grandchildren a pony. I can still remember the day he and my father took my brother and me to try some out. I was very happy riding an older trained pony around the ring but that is not the one we came home with. He bought a young colt that I named Champ. When we got home, my dad sat me on Champ's back and led me inside the house right into my Mother's living room. I can still hear him laughing at her fussing at him and saying, "That kid will be tired of that horse in six months." She had no clue that over fifty years later, I would still love them passionately. I also believe that my relationship with my horses through the years has kept me from making even more mistakes than I did.

When we moved to Mississippi, there were very few horse women in our area. In fact, there was not another one at my church. But through my real estate work, I met another agent who loved them as much as I did. She was older than me and her children were grown so she had been going to Tennessee on trail rides and invited me to come along. My boys were now in high school and this freed me to do so. I was hooked after this first trip and was so enthused about it that my husband decided to take up riding. We had been married almost twenty-three years and he had never before expressed an interest in riding. My friend also introduced me to Tennessee Walking Horses. They have a very special smooth gait. I had grown up riding quarter horses and Arabs. My horse was a quarter horse and both my boys learned to ride on her. She was the last present my father bought for me. In fact, at the time of this writing, she is almost twenty-six and I still have her. But once I started riding Tennessee Walkers, that was it for me. I bought myself a gaited horse and soon after an older one for my husband also. My precious quarter horse became the kid's horse. Through the years, whenever someone had a dream of riding a horse, she has been the one to make that come true. I did not realize it but this was the start of God taking me to ride the heights with Him.

I believe that God has a special love for the horses He created. His son is coming back riding one and that means there must be horses in heaven."

...then you will find your joy in the LORD, and I will cause you to ride in triumph on the heights of the land and to feast on the inheritance of your father Jacob." For the mouth of the LORD has spoken...
ISAIAH 58:14

I saw heaven standing open and there before me was a white horse, whose rider is called Faithful and True. With justice he judges and wages war.
REVELATION 19:11

Reluctance

When I was a teenager, God called me to surrender to Him in full-time ministry. When He did this, I thought if I said yes, it would mean He would send me to Africa or somewhere like that. So I told Him I would serve Him but I would become a teacher and help children. Both were incorrect. God did not call me to foreign missions and he did not call me to teach. He called me to surrender to Him and His will for my life. But in my fear that He would ask me to leave my home community I wanted to do it my way. Because of this, I was not very happy as a teacher. Oh, I did some good things and helped a few children, but I was not within the center of God's will for my life. I now call myself the "reluctant missionary."

God will find a way to get you where He wants you. But your attitude will determine if you go on a cruise ship, or in the belly of a fish like Jonah. I am afraid that much of my life I spent it as a Jonah. I have lived in six different states and more than one city in several of those. I look back sometimes and ask myself who I would have missed or what lesson learned or ministry blessing unknown if I had not lived in each of these areas. I also know that most of my suffering was because of my own stubborn rebellious heart desiring my own plans for my life instead of God's. But, I did come to a point where I was able to pray, "God make me willing to be willing." That was the point my life began to change and for the better.

*...because they rebelled against God's commands
and despised the plans of the Most High.*

PSALM 107:11

Stepping Out

With our now-regular trips to Tennessee for week-long trail rides, mine and my husband's relationship grew even stronger. The horses and the time we spent together with them were good for both of us and we developed relationships with other riders also. One year three trail-riding friends passed away close to each other. One of them was a special friend of ours who had died unexpectedly of a heart attack.

God kept speaking to my heart that it was time for me to be bolder in my faith and step out for Him. He wanted me to lead a memorial service at the next trail ride in honor of these friends. Many of the friends we rode with were Christians who loved the Lord but others had been wounded by the church and could be hostile to the Gospel and those presenting its message. You see, my reluctance was based on that old lie from Satan, that I must be accepted by certain others. I had to make the decision if this was what God wanted me to do, would I then seek to please Him or try to appease others? In spite of my fear, I decided to please God and lead the service. It was a small group of fifteen to twenty, but it was a success.

I did not understand but this was the start of God taking me outside of the traditional church. He was going to send me to search for His lost and scattered sheep. And in honor of those sheep, He gave me this poem to share and call to them.

My sheep wandered over all the mountains and on every high hill.
They were scattered over the whole earth,
and no one searched or looked for them.

EZEKIEL 34:6

Renegade Riders

Lined faces, from many a sun-kissed smile,
Leathered traces, born from many a mile.
Kindred hearts, knit by equine's love,
Freed spirits, gentled like a dove.
Breeze tossed manes, no walking canes for these
Blessed renegades of medicare.
Crossing mountains, barriers and streams,
The Journey is their prize.
They meet, no spoken words exchange,
What's written in their eyes.
The rhythm of the ride becomes their life's anthem,
Until their soul's Sure Guide
Calls them home to ride with Him.

Linda Foust Grajewski
November 2002

*"I saw heaven open and there before me
was a white horse, whose rider is called Faithful and True.*

With justice he judges and makes war. The armies of heaven were following him, riding on white horses and dressed in fine linen, white and clean."
REVELATION 19:11, 14

"The number of the mounted troops was two hundred million. I heard their number."
REVELATION 9:16

Wilderness

I did not share a lot to begin with about my college and early twenties because it seems to me that much of that time I just struggled. But maybe that is what most of us do during those years. I am reminded of a true story: A young man went to speak with his pastor and told him, "Pastor I have lost my faith." The pastor replied, "No son, you have lost your parent's faith. Now go out and get one of your own." Maybe that is what those years were about for me and maybe you also.

I did not have a car and so my parents and grandparents dropped me off. The college I choose was about four hours from my home. I still remember how I felt watching them drive off that day. I was so unsure, frightened, and lonely inside but trying hard not to reveal it on the outside. I did what many other students did by using food as comfort and packed on the pounds, which led to even more insecurity. I even visited our denominations student program on Sunday but no one spoke to me or included me in their group. No one contacted me afterward either. Maybe if someone had reached out, my college experience would have been different. But I acknowledge my part in this that I did not persevere and go back. I always try to encourage people when they visit a new church to go for at least a month before making a decision. Maybe this was just an excuse I used.

I grew up in a family where I was not encouraged to go to college or to advance myself professionally. In fact, my father said if I would become a nurse, he would help me go to the local nursing program or he had a job for me as a teller at the bank. Otherwise, I was on my own. He should have known better as he always said I was as stubborn as a mule. Why I have that dogged determination I do not know, except I was beginning even then to make the decision that I would believe my "Heavenly Father" and trust what He said in His Word to be true for me.

I persevered and graduated in four years. My father and mother came to my graduation and I was so proud. But when I came out to meet them, the only thing my Father said was, "Let's get out of here. I'm ready to go home." There was no celebration. No "I'm proud of you."

The human spirit can endure in sickness, but a crushed spirit who can bear?
PROVERBS 18:14

The Blessing

It would be many years later when I read the book *The Blessing* by Gary Smalley and John Trent that I began to understand and heal. The more I healed and the closer I came to God, the more determined I was to share this with my family and others. But my zeal, at times, approached legalism. I was just beginning to grow spiritually and so I wanted others to also.

There is a connection that God has with math. I don't understand it but if we just look in the Bible, we see numbers that He has given special significance to: 3, 7, and 40 are a few. Even some of the great events in the Bible have mathematical calculations. So I think it is important at this time to point something out; when we start first grade in math, we learn 2+2=4 and 3+3=6. Now for the vast majority of children, if they were given a calculus equation to solve at that point, it would not make any sense to them. But they are still doing math at 2+2=4. So it is with our spiritual lives that not everyone is on the same developmental level but that does not mean they are not a follower of Jesus Christ. Also, spirituality is developmental just as math is, and we must learn one precept to build upon to learn others. As I advanced with my mathematical education, I achieved the Algebra II and Geometry level but my oldest son does Calculus IV. Does this mean he is a better person than I am? No, it only means that he has a better understanding of that level of math.

Maybe spiritually you feel that your relationship with God is stuck at 2+2=4. Don't worry, I have been there. Sometimes I still feel like an adolescent spiritually when I am around some of my Christian friends but now I know it is alright and that I am right with God for I am His child.

"Truly I tell you, anyone who will not receive the kingdom of God like a little child will never enter it."
LUKE 18:17

Condemnation

This leads us to expose the next lie of Satan: "Those who fail are unworthy of love and deserve to be blamed and condemned." Many people who do not understand the disease of alcoholism and how it has generational consequences would condemn my father but God did not.

The last night we were at my parents, prior to my father's death, my youngest son, who was five at the time asked me, "Mommy, when I go to heaven will Papa be there too?" I told him that was a question he needed to ask his papa. He got out of bed and went to my parents' bedroom. After a few minutes, he came back and was very happy. He told me his papa had said that when he was a young man he had invited Jesus into his heart but he was ashamed because he had not always lived as he should and wanted my son to live better. What an amazing, gracious, and loving Heavenly Father we have to leave me with this assurance of my earthly father's destiny. You see my grandfather, my father's father, was an alcoholic also. My grandfather stopped drinking when I was a baby but he did not deal with this God's way, and it became a "high place of sacrifice" in his son's life. As I said before, 80 percent of the children of alcoholics themselves become alcoholics.

As I read the Bible and study the people God has used, I find no perfect people. But I find many that God says He loves even in failure.

If God could only use perfect people, then He never could use anyone at all, and that includes me. But more important is the fact that if we could ever be perfect people, then Jesus would have never had to die.

Therefore, there is now no condemnation for those who are in Christ Jesus…
ROMANS 8:1

This is love: not that we loved God, but that
he loved us and sent his Son as
an atoning sacrifice for our sins.
1 JOHN 4:10

Equipping

After I quit selling real estate I found myself with time on my hands to do other things. Several of the women in my church and I had been discussing and desiring more spiritual and fellowship opportunities. We went to our pastor and asked if we could start a Women's Ministry program and he blessed us in this effort. I was selected to be the director of the program. Not long after we went to him, he called me into his office to share some information he had just received. New Orleans Baptist Theological Seminary had just started a new degree program in Women's Ministry and he thought I might be interested in this. I told him I would pray and talk with my husband about it. God and my husband confirmed that this was for me. So I went and earned my Advanced Certification in Women's Ministry. This was by far the best thing I have ever been blessed to be a part of. The women who taught and participated in this program were and are incredible women of God.

It had been many years by this time since I had been in a classroom as a student and because I was still struggling mentally, I had my first severe panic attack the first day of class. I had to hold on to the side of the table and breathe and pray through it. I know this was an attack of the enemy to try and keep me from what God wanted to teach me. The things I learned and the relationships I was blessed with have sustained and helped me greatly. However, it still saddens me that there are so few opportunities for women leaders within the church and especially salaried positions. You see, at this time, I still was struggling to stay within the "safe boundaries of the traditional church, never fully understanding how unconventional I was and that God truly had created and was equipping me for a very different kind of work.

I took you from the ends of the earth, from its farthest corners I called you.
I said, 'You are my servant'; I have chosen you and have not rejected you.
ISAIAH 41:9

Study to shew thyself approved unto God,
a workman that needeth not to be ashamed,
rightly dividing the word of truth.
2 TIMOTHY 2:15

Beth Moore

As part of our Women's Ministry program, I led Bible studies by this precious woman of God's Word. Though I had been teaching in-depth Bible studies for years, no one spoke to me from God like she did. The study that had the most profound impact on my spiritual growth and life was, "A Heart Like His." I led that study at least three times and learned something new every time. This study really set me on the path of desiring His Heart. Before, I had more desired His Hand, or in other words, what He could and would do for me. Now I truly wanted the relationship.

Through this, Satan's lie of needing acceptance from others in order to feel good about myself was defeated. For in Christ we learn that we are completely forgiven, fully pleasing, and totally accepted by God. But this does not happen by simply participating in another Bible Study; it happens because we spend time alone with Him. The most important relationship in our lives is the one we have with our Creator. Being in intimate relationship, fellowshipping, and spending time alone with our Heavenly Father, is the most important thing we do. Satan will try and keep you too busy to do this for he knows without it we are powerless.

God is faithful, by whom ye were called unto the
fellowship of his Son Jesus Christ our Lord.
1 CORINTHIANS 1:9

May the grace of the Lord Jesus Christ, and the love of God,
and the fellowship of the Holy Spirit be with you all.
2 CORINTHIANS 13:14

We proclaim to you what we have seen and heard,
so that you also may have fellowship with us.
And our fellowship is with the Father and with his Son, Jesus Christ.
1 JOHN 1:3

Moving

Both boys were now in college and Joe and I felt a strong call to move to Tennessee. We rationalized that it put us closer to both our aging widowed mothers and into a climate that was healthier for me. I had suffered tremendously with my allergies in the New Orleans and south Mississippi area as pine trees and mold were killers to my system. We also wanted to be in an area of horse enthusiasts and have access to riding trails. It would take us over a year, however, to find a house. We started out looking in one area and ended up in another.

God has a way of getting us where He wants us. We actually made offers on two different places that were taken off the market when our agent called to present our offer and on a third that the seller would not compromise on the price. I almost gave up. In fact, I had made a disappointing trip to Tennessee looking at property in January 2003, and came home fully surrendering this dream to God. The next morning during my quiet time with Him I told Him if He wanted us to stay we would and would do it with joy, but that I was going to look in the computer listings one last time.

I found a home that had been listed while I was traveling. I called our agent to have him preview it and he called back excited saying he thought it was the one. I could not return for at least two weeks and during that time, the real estate market was hot in the Nashville area. But, I prayed and asked God that if this was His home for us to keep it. I went by myself and felt God's confirmation to buy this home. I put the contract on it without having sold our home in Mississippi. My husband actually came the next month and closed on the house without going inside first. Our home in south Mississippi sold just a few days after we closed on our new home, further confirming for us that we were where God wanted us to be. This was March of 2003. We moved me, our stuff, horses, and dog to Tennessee but Joe continued to live in south Mississippi and work in New Orleans. He was praying that the company he loved and had worked so faithfully for would eventually transfer him to Nashville.

The LORD knows all human plans; he knows that they are futile…
PSALM 94:11

Many are the plans in a person's heart, but it is the LORD's purpose that prevails.
PROVERBS 19:21

Was I fickle when I intended to do this?
Or do I make my plans in a worldly manner
so that in the same breath I say both "Yes, yes" and "No, no"?
2 CORINTHIANS 1:17

Promised Land

From my first night in our new home in Tennessee, I felt at home. Even though I was "home alone" I was never afraid. Because of my connection in the horse community, I already had a group of friends and found it very easy to make new ones. I also was invited and went to a church that first week promising to visit around before joining but the people and pastor were so great that I and my family joined that Easter Sunday in April.

Joe had four weeks of vacation and so he would use a day or two at a time to come for long weekends. The boys would come for holidays. Though lonely at times, we still believed this was part of God's plan for our lives. We lived this way until July 2005 when Joe accepted a position in the Nashville office with his company but it was a demotion and a greatly reduced salary. We questioned ourselves if we had heard correctly from God and searched our hearts and lives for areas of disobedience. But on August 29, 2005, one of the reasons we felt such a pull to move was confirmed as Katrina roared across the Mississippi Coast and brought destruction to New Orleans also. I was riveted to the news and prayed fervently for friends and people in those areas.

I had been questioning our decision to move to Tennessee. We had suffered some significant family situations and struggled financially. But this was confirmation to us that we were where God wanted us at this time. Picayune, Mississippi, the town where we had lived was the first high ground that did not experience significant flooding though it did sustain much wind damage. It was a refuge from the flooding for hundreds if not thousands of people. I was humbled in my spirit to think about all the new homes I had sold to people moving from Louisiana. God had used me in spite of my shortcomings to help prepare for the devastation and provide a safe place for others. He had provided a way for them to ride out the storm on the heights with Him.

The waves of death swirled about me; the torrents of destruction overwhelmed me.
2 SAMUEL 22:5

The LORD is my rock, my fortress and my deliverer; my God is my rock, in whom I take refuge, my shield and the horn of my salvation, my stronghold.
PSALM 18:2

Humility

It seems to me that most of my life God has been determined to develop this quality in me. He has done this by repeatedly placing me in situations that were not comfortable and sometimes allowed me to fall down and fail.

When I was young, we did not have an indoor bathroom until I was a teenager, and so one of my chores as a pre-teen was to take out the slop jar in the morning before catching the school bus. A slop jar is a ceramic pail that is used during the night in place of a toilet. My task was not a very pleasant one, as you can imagine.

One morning I was late and went running down the path to the outhouse to deliver the contents and fulfill my chore but the grass was wet and I slipped and fell, spewing the contents of the slop jar. Needless to say, I was very late for school that morning.

Another time, my pride was brought down was my freshman year in college. I was walking down a long flight of stairs, slipped, and fell. In those days, we did not wear slacks or jeans to school but dresses. My humiliation was further increased by the shredded pantyhose I had to wear the rest of the day.

One of my first days of teaching college I was leading in warm-up exercises and, you guessed it, I slipped and fell very hard on my rear. Everyone in the class was dead silent until I started laughing at myself. Yes, I am firmly convinced that God has firmly rooted humility in my life through humiliation, failure, and repeatedly falling down. But through this, He has also taught me not to take myself so serious, to laugh at my failures, and to let Him help me stand again whenever I fall.

We all will experience times of falling down in our lives, but we can make the decision of whether or not to stay down or allow God to take our hand and lift us up again. The only way to walk and not grow weary when we fall is to keep our eyes on Jesus who, for our sake, stayed on the cross so that we would not be defeated.

Do not gloat over me, my enemy! Though I have fallen, I will rise. Though I sit in darkness, the LORD will be my light.
MICAH 7:8

David said to Gad, "I am in deep distress. Let me fall into the hands of the LORD, for his mercy is very great; but do not let me fall into human hands."
1 CHRONICLES 21:13

The LORD upholds all who fall and lifts up all who are bowed down.
PSALM 145:14

Friend

Satan's third lie that held me in bondage and still holds so many others is: Those who fail are unworthy of love and deserve to be blamed and condemned. Yet Psalm 145 tells us that Jesus gave Judas the same miraculous power that He gave the other 11. He did not withhold His favor because He knew that Judas would fail. This is a really hard thing for us to get a hold of. Culturally, and in our churches, Judas has been vilified and his name used for the worst of betrayers. Jesus went even further. For on the night the soldiers came into the garden to arrest Him Jesus called Judas "friend."

This implies to us that Jesus knew fully what Judas was doing; it was not a surprise. "What a friend we have in Jesus" is the line from an old song that many of us know. But in its familiarity, have we missed its power? What condemnation or blame have you been holding onto? Is it yourself that you are seeking to punish, or someone else? I punished myself for years because I failed to meet my expectations of myself as a Christ follower. Do you see in that previous sentence what my focus was? It wasn't Christ but self. To be included in the friends of Jesus means that we all fall short at times. We need to learn how to let the blood of Jesus cover and rub out mistakes and not rub them in. Please do not think that by my saying these things that I am excusing sin or giving others the right to cause harm or pain. We will talk later about healthy boundaries and accountability. This is about our learning to be Jesus' friend and that any friend of Jesus is a friend of mine. And that by the finished work of Jesus, we are "deeply loved by God, completely forgiven, fully pleasing, totally accepted and a new creation—complete in Christ." (Dr. Robert McGee)

As the song goes, "What a friend we have in Jesus, all our sin and grief to bear, what a privilege to carry everything to the Lord in prayer."

He called his twelve disciples to him and gave them authority to drive out evil spirits and to heal every disease and sickness.
MATTHEW 10:1

Jesus replied, "Do what you came for, friend."
Then the men stepped forward, seized Jesus and arrested him.
MATTHEW 26:50

Little Gifts

My love of horses started when I was five years old. One year my parents gave me a painting of a mare with her foal lying at her feet. That painting moved with me from home to home and state to state through the years. I treasured it. But when my boys were teens a group of them were rough housing one day and knocked it off the wall. The broken glass shredded it and I had to throw it away. I looked for a copy of that painting every-where—in junk stores, antique vendors, and yard sales for years. But about ten years later at a time I desperately needed my Heavenly Father to encourage me, it came to me.

I was working as a mortgage loan officer and was visiting a local real estate broker and that painting was hanging on her wall. I commented on it and told her my story. She looked astonished and said, "I have another copy at home. It is yours." That precious lady gave me that painting and it is now hanging in my home again. This happened at a very critical time in my life. God knew I needed a touch from Him to remind me of His stead-fast love and that I needed to know that He cared even about the smallest things in my life. Many times over the next few years, I would look at that painting and remember no matter what was happening, God could and would sustain and restore.

I have a friend that calls these small gifts "little happies." I like the word I learned in Louisiana: lagniappe. Lagniappe means a little something extra. That is what God is and does in our lives. When He restores, it is not to the condition that it was previously, but He does a little something extra.

Restore to me the joy of your salvation
and grant me a willing spirit, to sustain me.
PSALM 51:12

Though you have made me see troubles,
many and bitter, you will restore my life again;
from the depths of the earth you will again bring me up.
PSALM 71:20

After Job had prayed for his friends, the LORD restored his fortunes
and gave him twice as much as he had before.
JOB 42:10

Perspective

Once when my children were young I got the bright idea of trying to help them learn the concept of looking at things from different perspectives. So I got out the ladder and we climbed to the top of our house and sat on the roof talking and waving at people passing by. What a difference the twelve to fourteen feet made in our view! As we talked, I pointed this out to the boys and told them that in life, when bad things happen, we can sometimes be overwhelmed. But if we take a step back and seek higher ground, we get an entirely different understanding of what is going on. The "higher ground" we should seek is by God's side and in His Word. Sometimes we can almost feel as if we are drowning in our troubles but when we learn to stand on God's Word and trust His character, we can survive the flood that overwhelms others.

So many people have the misconception that becoming a Christ follower means health, wealth, and prosperity. A false ideology has arisen that professes you will have all your needs met and no adversity in this life. Nothing could be farther from the truth. Your adversity could and probably will increase the more you seek to become like Jesus.

Yes, we all need to be able to get a different perspective of things in our own lives and of events around us in the world today. We need God's view and we can only achieve that by being rooted firmly in His Word.

But since they have no root, they last only a short time.
When trouble or persecution comes because of the word, they quickly fall away.
MATTHEW 13:21

Therefore, among God's churches we boast about your perseverance and faith
in all the persecutions and trials you are enduring.
2 THESSALONIANS 1:4

Now if we are children, then we are heirs—
heirs of God and co-heirs with Christ,
if indeed we share in his sufferings
in order that we may also share in his glory.
ROMANS 8:17

Fruit

Years ago when we lived within the city limits of Picayune, I had a single pear tree in my backyard. South Mississippi is hot and humid in the summer. The sweat would drip from me even watering the flowers on my porch. I never did a thing to that pear tree. I did not prune it, fertilize it, treat it for pests, nothing to cause it to bear fruit, but bear fruit in abundance it did. For years, I had prayed scripture in my life and asked God to give me fruit from the work I did for Him. You see, I still needed to see results my way. One summer God would teach me a great object lesson through that tree.

As I said, I did nothing to help or cause that tree to bear fruit but it was loaded. The branches were so heavy they touched the ground. I went out and started picking the fruit from that tree. As I worked, sweated, and grumbled God spoke to my heart and said, "Child, you want fruit, I will give you fruit, but I will not pick it, can it, and put it in your pantry. Fruit takes work." I mistakenly thought that fruit was the result of my work. No, fruit is the work of the Holy Spirit. My work is to harvest that fruit.

Henry Blackaby in his book *Experiencing God* has said to look where God is working and join up. So I picked twelve large grocery bags of fruit from that tree, which I shared with friends and others in that community. I was able to bless others because of the fruit God provided and the humble work I did.

Then he said to his disciples, "The harvest is plentiful but the workers are few."
MATTHEW 9:37

In the same way, the gospel is bearing fruit and growing throughout the whole world—just as it has been doing among you since the day you heard it and truly understood God's grace.
COLOSSIANS 1:6

Don't you have a saying, 'It's still four months until harvest'?
I tell you, open your eyes and look at the fields! They are ripe for harvest.
JOHN 4:35

Giants

When I entered the sixth grade I was the second tallest person in our class. I also weighed as much or more than I do now. In other words, I had reached my full physical growth at that time, but the rest of my peers had not. When my other peers were slender and small, I was tall and muscular. I have a picture taken then with my brother who was a year younger and my cousin who was the same age. I look like a giant next to them. This caused me to have a distorted body image that prevailed for years. Once we get something rooted into our brain, it takes a lot of work to change that. This is Satan's fourth and maybe greatest lie: "I am what I am. I cannot change. I am hopeless."

Do our thoughts reveal what we really believe? Only if they are allowed to take root and grow there. We cannot help sometimes the thoughts that come to us, but we can make the decision to look at them through the lens of God's Word. We can then train ourselves to recognize, reject, and replace untrue or ungodly thoughts with God's Truth. We can truly develop the mind of Christ in ourselves. Or as Dr. Robert McGee says, "Our thoughts are seldom neutral. They either reflect beliefs based on God's Word or on the world's values. The Lord can give us the perception we need to identify the source of our thoughts and determine if they are of Him or not."

The media driven culture has set up impossible and unnatural standards of beauty. This has caused an increase in mental disorders, especially among young girls. Too high a value is set upon outward appearance instead of qualities that are of real and lasting value.

What size am I you may be asking? I am 5'6" tall and wear a size 6–8, hardly a giant.

What giants in your life need to be demolished by God's Word today?

We demolish arguments and every pretension that sets itself up against the knowledge of God, and we take captive every thought to make it obedient to Christ.
2 CORINTHIANS 10:5

But the LORD said to Samuel, "Do not consider his appearance or his height, for I have rejected him. The LORD does not look at the things people look at. People look at the outward appearance, but the LORD looks at the heart."
1 SAMUEL 16:7

Death

My first encounter with this part of life was when I was in sixth grade. My grandmother was diagnosed with cancer. One day I came upon my father and grandfather crying. I asked them if Granny was going to die and they said no she was just very sick. A short time later, I was spending the night with my aunt and overheard her on the phone the next morning discussing my grandmother's death. I asked her if Granny died. She said yes. I think I was in shock for quite a while. I did not want to accept this, nor the fact that my father and grandfather had lied to me. Maybe they were in denial but at that age, I did not understand those things.

My next encounter was in junior high and it was just as difficult. We had to share lockers at school and one day my locker mate did not come to school. I tried calling her several times over the next few weeks but no one ever answered or called me back. Then one of the teachers told us she had leukemia. My friend died and I was given the task of cleaning her things out of our locker. No one counseled with me or spoke about her death. I struggled with these things for years, maybe even experiencing what is now called "survivors guilt." Why did this happen to them? Why have I been so blessed?

There are many questions in life that truly have no answer. We can waste our time, energy, and resources on them or on being about the business of living. I finally came to the resolution in my own heart and mind that God did have a plan and purpose, even if I did not like it at times. Death is inevitable for all of us. It is that final door we must walk through. But now I am sure of the fact that my Lord, Savior, and Heavenly Father is waiting on the other side. I will also see my granny and my friend again.

I no longer fear this appointment, nor look at death in the same way I did as a child. This does not mean I will not grieve when someone I love dies, but I do not grieve as those who have no hope. We are spiritual beings living temporarily in physical bodies. Death sets us free from these confines. It is not the end, but the beginning.

When the perishable has been clothed with the imperishable, and the mortal with immortality, then the saying that is written will come true: "Death has been swallowed up in victory."
1 CORINTHIANS 15:54

From one man he made all the nations, that they should inhabit the whole earth; and he marked out their appointed times in history and the boundaries of their lands.
ACTS 17:26

Just as people are destined to die once, and after that to face judgment...
HEBREWS 9:27

Impact

During my years of selling real estate, I had some very disappointing experiences. What made some of them even more so was that they were with professing Christians. One day, a Christian friend of mine who was also a real estate agent told me I never let my physical life impact my spiritual life. He knew I was struggling with this. I listened to him, went home, and thought about what he had said. The next morning when I was reading my Bible and having my quiet time with God, He spoke to my heart on this issue. If you are asking the wrong question, you will always get the wrong answer. The question we as Christians in the world should be asking ourselves is: Is my spiritual life impacting my physical life?

Making a living can be tough for most of us and we can get caught up in trying to provide for our families and maintain a certain standard of living. But while we are doing so, we must try and remember the life we are building that others see. I am sure I have disappointed many along the way and have fallen short of their expectations. But I daily run to the Father and ask for His forgiveness and help. I truly want my spiritual life to impact my physical life.

The longer we walk this way daily with God, the more we begin to see that there is no distinction between the spiritual and the physical, no difference between the secular and the holy. A life lived in relationship with

God through His Son Jesus Christ empowered by the Holy Spirit cannot help but impact the physical world.

You, my brothers and sisters, were called to be free. But do not use your freedom to indulge the flesh; rather, serve one another humbly in love.
GALATIANS 5:13

Whatever happens, conduct yourselves in a manner worthy of the gospel of Christ.
PHILIPPIANS 1:27

Gossip

One day when I was in eighth grade, not long after making the decision to surrender my heart and life to Jesus Christ, I went into the bathroom at school and came upon a group of my friends laughing. I asked them, "What's so funny?" One of the girls turned around and replied, "It's a joke but you wouldn't like it you're a Christian." She did not say this as a compliment but as a jabbing insult meant to hurt and exclude me from their group. In fact, the rest of the girls laughed and closed their circle leaving me on the outside. I was wounded but said nothing and walked away.

Another time when I was a senior in high school, a classmate, who was not a professing Christian told me, "Linda I have noticed that you do not gossip like the rest of the girls." I now know that these were two of the greatest compliments I have ever received. I wish that they were true of me now but over the years, I must confess I have indulged in gossip and far too often. I have been convicted by the Holy Spirit of my participation and even initiation of this. It is always to tear others down in an attempt to make myself look better. But I want my words to build others up and not tear them down. To bring unity, not division.

There is a reason that Jesus is called "the Word." Our words are powerful; they are long lived in the minds, hearts, and spirits of other people. I cannot go back and gather up all the gossip I have spread about others but I can dedicate the rest of my life to stopping this destructive vice and replacing it with words of healing and blessing.

A perverse person stirs up conflict, and a gossip separates close friends.
PROVERBS 16:28

They have become filled with every kind of wickedness, evil, greed and depravity. They are full of envy, murder, strife, deceit and malice. They are gossips...
ROMANS 1:29

For I am afraid that when I come I may not find you as I want you to be, and you may not find me as you want me to be. I fear that there may be discord, jealousy, fits of rage, selfish ambition, slander, gossip, arrogance and disorder.
2 CORINTHIANS 12:20

Do not let any unwholesome talk come out of your mouths, but only what is helpful for building others up according to their needs, that it may benefit those who listen.
EPHESIANS 4:29

Meekness

*"There is something about the outside of a horse that
is good for the inside of a man."*
—Winston Churchill

This is perhaps one of the most misunderstood concepts not only in
the Christian community, but in our culture as a whole. This word has
become characterized as a weak, fearful individual but nothing could be
farther from the truth. The Greek word for meekness is *prautes*. It is best
defined as gentleness and was most often used to describe a horse that
was trained and submissive to its rider. I love my horses but am aware
that these one thousand-pound animals could at any time seriously injure
or even kill me. They must be submissive and obedient to me, accept me
as their leader, and trust me. In other words, we must be in a relationship
where only one of us is in charge and that is me. Without this relationship, not only is that horse useless, he is dangerous. That is the same way
we are. When we try to be our own herd leader and go our own way we
are dangerous to ourselves and others.

The picture of meekness that I best understand is a horse's strength
under the control of the rider. Often the first question someone asks about
a horse is, is he gentle? No one would ever say a horse is weak. In fact, we

even designate the power of an engine by the amount of horsepower it has. On a horse that is gentle, submissive, and trained I can ride the high places safely. In other words, I can go places and do things that I could not do on my own.

When I was young, my father would compare me to a wild gangling colt and that is just how I was. But now I regularly do a check of my spirit with a picture in my mind of being bridled and the reins in God's hands, knowing that when I am filled and empowered by the Holy Spirit, I can go places and accomplish things that would be impossible on my own.

But the meek will inherit the land and enjoy peace and prosperity.
PSALM 37:11

But in your hearts revere Christ as Lord. Always be prepared to give an answer to everyone who asks you to give the reason for the hope that you have. But do this with gentleness and respect...
1 PETER 3:15

Baking Cookies

When my children were small I regularly let them stand on a stool or in a chair and help me make cookies in the kitchen. It was usually very messy and I would have a lot to clean up afterwards. I could have made those cookies much more quickly, easier, and neater by myself and with much less of a mess to clean afterwards. So why did I let the boys help me? There were several reasons but the most important was I wanted them to spend time with me. I wanted to build our relationship. That is the same way our Heavenly Father is. He wants to spend time with us and to grow our relationship with Him. Sometimes He will do this by letting us help Him do a work that is messy and has a lot to clean up afterwards. But there are lessons we can only learn by doing this with Him.

Maybe you thought what you were involved in would be easy and it has turned out to be a big mess. Maybe you are feeling overwhelmed and disappointed because things did not turn out the way you planned. I have found out that many times, God has a different lesson plan than we do. We may think the lesson is about making perfect cookies while His plan is about growing our relationship with Him and others.

Often when we are in a mess, we are tempted to just give up and walk away, for it seems overwhelming to us. But just as I did not leave my children to clean up the mess in our kitchen by themselves, God will not abandon us either. He will come right into the middle of our mess and find a way to turn it into a blessing.

But the plans of the LORD stand firm forever,
the purposes of his heart through all generations.
PSALM 33:11

Commit to the LORD whatever you do, and he will establish your plans...
PROVERBS 16:3

Many are the plans in a person's heart,
but it is the LORD's purpose that prevails.
PROVERBS 19:21

"For I know the plans I have for you," declares the LORD, "plans to prosper
you and not to harm you, plans to give you hope and a future."
JEREMIAH 29:11

Anger

I have always had a problem with anger. That is mainly because I have a control issue. In the past, I struggled with this as many co-dependent people do. We have an illusion of being in control of ourselves, others, and situations. One way that God helped to tear down this destructive high place in my life was by letting me have a new home constructed. Having a new home built was one of the most frustrating experiences of my life. I would go over every evening after work to check on the progress and clean up at least some of the mess from the day. Over and over I would discover something that had been broken but no one would admit responsibility and we would end up having to pay to have it fixed. Then one day, it rained and I came into the biggest mess inside the house. Boxes, construction debris, and mud were everywhere. As I worked to clean the mess, the angrier I became.

I piled the boxes in the backyard and proceeded to burn them. The anger inside of me burned much like the flames from the burning boxes. Suddenly, a strong wind came up and blew the fire and boxes toward the back of the house. I was shocked as I ran to get the hose and put the fire out, slipping and sliding in the mud all the way.

After the fire was out, I sat on the back porch with the boys. I was wet, covered in mud, and disgusted with myself as we surveyed the damage. The heat from the fire had melted the vinyl on the ceiling of the porch and part of the back of the house. I told my sons, here is another lesson your Mother has taught you, anger can become like a raging uncontrollable fire, destroying everything around it. I was angry because I could not control the actions of others but God taught me that sometimes I did not even control myself very well, and that some things are out of our control all together.

In my anger, I almost burned our new home down. But how many times in anger do we destroy our spiritual homes and also damage the spirits of others around us? Anger can be a motivating force to correct some things, but it is more often destructive and does not produce the righteousness that God desires in us.

'The LORD is slow to anger, abounding in love
and forgiving sin and rebellion."
NUMBERS 14:18

But you, Lord, are a compassionate and gracious God, slow to anger,
abounding in love and faithfulness.
PSALM 86:15

...because human anger does not produce the righteousness that God desires.
JAMES 1:20

Money

Did you know that Jesus had more to say about money than any other topic? I think it is because He knew what a difficult time we would all have with it. So many people believe their value and the value of others is in how much money they have and the things they own. In our culture, we have to have money to buy a home, food, clothing, electricity, water, transportation…the list is almost endless. But as I have gotten older, I ask myself the question, do I own these things or do they own me? How much time do I give to taking care of stuff and making money to buy more stuff? We have laughed and cried many times over money or the lack of it in our lives. But my husband and I have seen God provide over and over again. We have always had our needs met and our bills paid, even if we did not have an abundance of overflow for every want. God has even provided for us to have some to share with others and for His Kingdom purposes.

God knows me far better than I know myself and I think if I had been blessed with money I would not be as dependent on Him. I would look to money to meet my needs. I heard it said that if money can solve your problem, you don't have a problem. We certainly see evidence all around us of the truth of this statement. Money can give you options, but it cannot make you happy. Money can free you up to do ministry, but it cannot buy you a joy-filled relationship with God and others.

Money is a tool to help build the foundation of our lives, but it is not the foundation. It is neither evil nor good in itself, but it is how we use and relate to it that affects us. Every kind of evil comes when we love money and things but use people. Having an abundance of money is a good thing when our hearts are right about this issue and when it is used as a tool to further the Kingdom of Christ and to meet the needs of others.

Whoever loves money never has enough; whoever loves wealth is never satisfied with their income. This too is meaningless.
ECCLESIASTES 5:10

"No one can serve two masters. Either you will hate the one and love the other, or you will be devoted to the one and despise the other. You cannot serve both God and money."
LUKE 16:13

In this way they will lay up treasure for themselves as a firm foundation for the coming age, so that they may take hold of the life that is truly life.
1 TIMOTHY 6:19

Accidents

Early one morning in 2001, my husband and I were awakened by a phone call. It was my dear friend's niece calling me from Houston to tell me her cousin, my friend's son, had been killed that night in a car accident. I told her to tell Laura to hold on, I was on my way. While I packed, my husband called and made a reservation on a flight out of New Orleans for me. I also called another friend in Houston who agreed to pick me up at the airport and take me to Laura's. We received that call at 6 a.m. and I was on my friend's doorstep in Houston before noon. I helped with all the arrangements and stayed with her for several days before returning home.

My husband picked me up at the airport in New Orleans and drove me home. As we pulled into our driveway, there sat my youngest son's car covered in a tarp. They had not told me that on the way home from church Sunday, my son had been hit by a drunk driver and it had totaled his car. That voice spoke to me again and said, "Stop being afraid. Nothing will happen to you or your children until my hand is removed and when it is time to come home." I cannot say I have never had a moment of fear again but I can say that is all it lasts—a moment. Fear no longer has a hold on me. I know there are no accidents in my life that take God by surprise. I did not know it then but I needed this lesson to prepare me for what I would face in the years to come. Why God took my friend's son and yet spared mine, I do not know. I do know that my friend's son was ready. The evidence we found in his room afterward of his relationship with God was amazing in one so young.

The paradox of the free will of man versus the sovereignty of God is one we may not understand until we are with Him, but I do know that nothing ever takes Him by surprise. He is not shaken by world events, disasters, tragedies, or accidents. I have often thought what will I leave behind for others to discover in my room and life? What will you leave behind?

In him we were also chosen, having been predestined according to the plan of him who works out everything in conformity with the purpose of his will, in order that we, who were the first to put our hope in Christ, might be for the praise of his glory.
EPHESIANS 1:11–12

When a trumpet sounds in a city, do not the people tremble?
When disaster comes to a city, has not the LORD caused it?
AMOS 3:6

Weeds

I hate weeds. I am always at war with the weeds in my garden. I pull them, I put growth inhibiters on them, I put mulch on them, everything I can do but they keep coming back. God has taught me some great lessons while pulling weeds. One was the fact that I needed to get to the root of the weed to keep it from coming back. That is the same way with sin and character defects in my own life. I have to get to the root of the problem and replace it with God's Word.

One day when I was angrily pulling weeds in my flowerbed, God spoke to my heart and said, "Child, I did not make you a weed puller in other people's lives, I made you a seed planter." Ouch! I had been spending far too much time and energy as a weed puller rather than seed planter. When all of our time, strength, and energy go toward pulling weeds, there is nothing left for seed planting. Jesus gave us clear directions concerning this but I had either been ignoring them in favor of my own, or just did not understand.

"'No,' he answered, 'because while you are pulling
the weeds, you may uproot the wheat with them.'"
MATTHEW 13:29

Let both grow together until the harvest.
MATTHEW 13:30

It is clear from God's Word that the reason we are not to spend our time on pulling weeds is not to protect the weeds, but to protect the wheat. How much damage had my critical judgmental spirit caused? I have resolved to be a Johnny Appleseed for the Word of God; to plant it wherever I go and trust the Lord of the Harvest with the results.

THE JOHNNY APPLESEED SONG (1774–1845)

Oh, the Lord's been good to me.
And so I thank the Lord
For giving me the things I need:
The sun, the rain and the appleseed;
Oh, the Lord's been good to me.
Oh, and every seed I sow
Will grow into a tree.
And someday there'll be apples there
For everyone in the world to share.
Oh, the Lord is good to me.

Gifts

The hardest that Jesus ever was on anyone was the story of the talents. You can find this in Matthew 25. To one person he gave five talents, to one he gave two, and to another he gave one talent. The first two individuals used their talents and were able to present them along with the increase to the Master when he returned, but the third with only one talent buried it out of fear. Jesus called him "a wicked and slothful servant." He did not treat anyone else with the big sins this way—not the woman in adultery, not the thief on the cross, not David when he committed murder. So why was He so hard on this man? I believe it is because God wants us to use whatever gift He gives us to build His Kingdom and bless others. When we are not operating in our gift because of fear, we are not living by faith.

Then he brought forward the tribe of Benjamin,
clan by clan, and Matri's clan was chosen.
Finally Saul son of Kish was chosen.
But when they looked for him, he was not to be found.
So they inquired further of the LORD,
"Has the man come here yet?"
And the LORD said,
"Yes, he has hidden himself among the baggage."
SAMUEL 10:21–22

What is holding you back? Have you been hiding among the baggage in your life?

I know I did. Maybe it is time for a house cleaning to get rid of the baggage and make room for the Holy Spirit to live in you. I want no closed doors with old baggage to hide in. The funny thing is God knows all about it anyway. We cannot hide it or hide ourselves from Him. Locked doors and baggage don't keep God out; they only keep us in. If you notice in the scripture, it was God who told them where Saul was hiding. I may only be a one-talent person, but I am going to put that to work. How about you?

Prophecy

Being a perfectionist caused me to tend to be legalistic. I justified it by saying I had the gift of prophesy. The word prophecy means to "bubble up, to flow forth, or to cause to drop like rain." To someone struggling in a desert time, that sounds very refreshing, but I am afraid that many times I operated more like a volcano spewing fire and burning lava on my victims. This gift also gives one a very clear vision to see things as either black or white, not gray. When operating in this gift by the power of the Holy Spirit, it is a very useful and helpful gift, giving clear direction and insight for others.

But how do you know if this is from God? According to 1 Corinthians 14:3, this gift should be for our strengthening, encouragement, and comfort, and should lead us to the Word of God.

Whether you turn to the right or to the left, your ears will hear a voice behind you, saying, "This is the way; walk in it."
ISAIAH 30:21

Dear friends, do not believe every spirit,
but test the spirits to see whether they are from God,
because many false prophets have gone out into the world.
1 JOHN 4:1

Many times in the past, I may have thought I meant well in my harsh judgment, but I was operating out of my own flesh and not this gift. The result was not the promise of 1 Corinthians; instead I was cutting off the ears of my listeners and wounding their spirits. I was much like another disciple quick to draw my sword in righteous anger.

And one of them struck the servant of the high priest,
cutting off his right ear.
LUKE 22:50

But Jesus answered, "No more of this!"
And he touched the man's ear and healed him.
LUKE 22:51

The Word of God will accomplish the purpose He sets for it in our lives, and the Holy Spirit living in us will change us. I am grateful I am not what I once was, but also that I am not who I will become.

The Spirit of the LORD will come upon you in power,
and you will prophesy with them; and
you will be changed into a different person.
1 SAMUEL 10:6

Rejection

As I shared before, I have done a bit of moving in my life having now lived in six states and twelve cities. In each of those, the task of finding a church home and family fell to me. When we moved to Slidell, it was the Christmas Season. We made our first visit to a local church and really enjoyed the Sunday services. They were having a Christmas program and fellowship that evening. Joe had some work to do at his new office so I decided to go and take the boys. The program was wonderful and we went to their fellowship hall afterward. I had brought something to share and placed it on the food table. I saw another table where a number of women had placed their purses and belongings to save a place, so I did the same and then helped the boys serve their plates and sit down at a table of other men and boys. When I walked over to the women's table, all of the seats except mine were taken but a young woman in front of me picked up my purse and asked whose purse it was. When I said mine, she handed it to me and sat down in my place. None of the other women acknowledged me in any way. No one invited me to get another chair, nothing, they totally ignored me. I went and sat with the boys, ate, and went home never to return to that church.

If I had been lost or a more immature Christian, I would have rejected Christianity as just a bunch of hypocrites. Fortunately by now I had enough maturity to try another church in the area and it was wonderful. God used this rejection to get us to the place He wanted us with a church family that was and still is a blessing to us, as we have kept many relationships we made there through the years.

Offer hospitality to one another without grumbling.
1 PETER 4:9

And the LORD told him: "Listen to all that the people are saying to you; it is not you they have rejected, but they have rejected me as their king."
1 SAMUEL 8:7

As I have matured in my relationship with God, I have come to understand the rejection I experienced from these women better. Does it hurt less when I experience rejection now? Yes he does, for now I see it through the lens of God's Word and know I have not experienced anything He has not. I may be rejected by people but I am **chosen by God** and precious to Him. So are you!

He then began to teach them that the Son of Man must suffer many things and be rejected by the elders, chief priests and teachers of the law, and that he must be killed and after three days rise again.
MARK 8:31

As you come to him, the living Stone—rejected by men but chosen by God and precious to him...
1 PETER 2:4

Hospitality

Joe and I have now lived in eighteen different residences. Some of these were temporary apartments while we were waiting to get into our new home but ten were homes that we lived in for months to years at a time and all were in nice neighborhoods. In all of these moves, only once did someone knock on my door welcome me. She was new also. In fact, she knocked on my door because she saw the cross on it and desperately needed a friend, having just returned to the states after living abroad for eleven years. We are still the dearest of friends. I share this to tell others not to sit at home alone waiting but get out and get involved. First find a good Bible teaching Bible believing church and get involved. Join a ladies Bible Study or find a hobby group. But don't isolate. I write this also to encourage Christians to knock on that new neighbor's door, take a meal, take information about your church and community, and show them Christian hospitality. You just may make a friend not only for life, but for eternity.

When my friend knocked on my door that day, I opened it in hospitality not knowing what a blessing she would prove to be to me through the years.

...and is well known for her good deeds,
such as bringing up children, showing hospitality,

washing the feet of the saints, helping those in trouble
and devoting herself to all kinds of good deeds.
1 TIMOTHY 5:10

I am a friend to all who fear you,
to all who follow your precepts.
PSALM 119:63

Brokenness

Thanksgiving 2003 began the most difficult journey for us, one that many would not have survived, and one I would not wish on my worst enemy. I am convinced that the reason we made it was because I fell upon the stone in brokenness.

When my youngest son came home from college for the Thanksgiving Holliday we were hit full force by his illness. I did not think he was capable of going back to finish the semester, but he insisted. Christmas was even worse. I called his coach who was also the Dean of Students and he said that he was on academic probation but they had to let him continue for the next semester. He had gone from making a 3.5 GPA his freshman year to D's and F's that fall semester of his sophomore year. He returned to school in January but his condition worsened and his coach finally called and said we needed to come take him to the doctor. I drove the seven hours to where he was going to school and we got him into the hospital. There one of the medical staff told me that I just had to face facts: my son was very ill and we would just have to give up our hopes and dreams for him. The pain was almost unbearable, a thousand tiny knives piercing my heart. But I made the decision not to believe this "expert."

My son came home to Tennessee to live with us here and I began the process of doctors, hospitals, and research. I left no stone unturned. I am sure I have studied and learned enough to have earned a PhD. But as I was running to the medical field for help, I was also enlisting every prayer warrior I could to pray for his healing. I also had a friend, gifted in this area, to anoint him with oil and we laid hands on him and prayed. We finally met the right doctor and he told me, "I am going to give you back your son," and praise God, he did. But also my son stopped being in denial and took ownership and responsibility for his illness and started doing the things that were necessary for him to remain healthy. I do not share a lot of this process because it is my son's story to share, not mine. I am only going to share how it impacted my life and how God used it for my good. This entire process of healing would take over five years.

"Therefore I tell you that the kingdom of
God will be taken away from you and given
to a people who will produce its fruit.
He who falls on this stone will be broken to pieces,
but he on whom it falls will be crushed."
MATTHEW 21:43-44

The LORD is nigh unto them that are of a broken heart;
and saveth such as be of a contrite spirit.
PSALM 34:18

He healeth the broken in heart,
and bindeth up their wounds.
PSALM 147:3

Despair

When my son's illness was at its worst, I felt as if we were in a war battle and he had been wounded. It was my job to get him to the medics and safety. I had to pick him up and carry him off that battlefield with bombs and mortar fire and at times, a thick haze of confusing smoke. We ran this way and that seeking to get out of the battle and to safety until I was completely exhausted and in despair, but it was then that God took over.

I did not give up easily. I did not let go and let God. God had to wrench my son out of my closed fists. The way out of the battle was not the one I would have chosen, but I learned God's ways are not ours. We want things easy, neat, and free. But sometimes they are messy, difficult, and costly.

"Can you fathom the mysteries of God?
Can you probe the limits of the Almighty?
They are higher than the heavens—what can you do?
They are deeper than the depths of the grave—what can you know?
Their measure is longer than the earth and wider than the sea."

JOB 11:7–9

Yes, my son's path to healing was very costly, very messy, and very difficult, but God came right into the middle of it all with us and made a way where others had said there was none. He did not rescue us from this valley of despair but helped us walk through it to be able to ride the heights with Him. He also used this to better equip us to serve others and walk with them through their valley. At my times of deepest despair, I would cry out to God, claiming His promises. I asked Him to please not let us go through this without being able to use it for good not only for ourselves but to help others also.

...and provide for those who grieve in Zion—to bestow on them a crown of beauty instead of ashes, the oil of gladness instead of mourning, and a garment of praise instead of a spirit of despair. They will be called oaks of righteousness, a planting of the LORD for the display of his splendor.
ISAIAH 61:3

Now He has truly given us a garment of praise instead of despair and we are a planting of the Lord for the display of His splendor. Our son is now a college senior and doing awesome, but he is the Lord's planting and work, not mine. In my brokenness and despair, I have been set free from any pride or self-righteous accomplishment. For I know that it is ALL the Lord's work. He just lets me come along for the ride.

Pieces

When I fell upon the "stone" I felt like humpty dumpty and that all the king's horses and all the king's men could not put me back together again. But the King of kings and Lord of lords could and did. Before, much like a coin, I was stamped with the image of man. But when He puts us back together in our brokenness, it is to stamp us with His image. He restores us not to the person we were, but to the person He created and desires us to be. That is what **brokenness is about—not the pieces but the wholeness** He brings through it.

Then God said, "Let us make man in our image…"
GENESIS 1:26

The process of God remaking us in His image is often painful and long but it is worth it. It is never His desire to crush us into dust, but if we harden our hearts, that is what happens. Another curious thing about brokenness is the shared blessings that come from it. When the bread was broken it was useful to feed many! Left whole it was nice to look at and may have smelled great, but it brought no nourishment to others. Another curious thing about brokenness is while before there was only one, now there is a shared abundance.

While they were eating, Jesus took bread, gave thanks and broke it, and gave it to his disciples, saying, "Take and eat; this is my body."
MATTHEW 26:26

...and the disciples picked up twelve basketfuls of broken pieces of bread and fish.
MARK 6:43

There were twelve disciples and from five loaves that were broken, God restored twelve extra baskets, one for each. Not only did everyone eat their fill then, but they were blessed with an abundance to share with others later. Maybe you are in that place of brokenness and just do not see how it is possible for God to restore and use you. Yes, being broken is messy and painful but it becomes love multiplied. It is how God transforms us from only feeding ourselves to be able to feed others.

Mockers

I am not the only one who has felt the painful scorn of mockers. But it is one thing that God used to bring me to brokenness and then restored me to wholeness in Christ Jesus. You see, He also felt that pain.

While still struggling with my own pride and self-righteousness, God gave me another poem to minister to me and to share with others.

RIDE WITH THE SON

Ride for the Son, I made my cry,
When trails were wide and straight.
But then they led through mountains high
So steep, on rocky ledges fell
While in the precipice I heard the mockers call my name.
T'was then I knew was not enough
To ride alone for Him,
But with Him I must ride.
The only safety would be found
By riding at His side.
Ride with the Son rose from my lips.
He took me by the hand
And gently lifted me to ride

With Him now instead.
Through valleys long or mountains high
Worn paths or new ones make.
He is the "Trail Boss" that I choose
To ride with all my days.

His pleasure is not in the strength of the horse,
nor his delight in the legs of a man;
the Lord delights in those who fear him.
Who put their hope in his unfailing love.
PSALM 147:10–11

After they had mocked him, they took off the robe
and put his own clothes on him.
Then they led him away to crucify him.
MATTHEW 7:31

In the same way the chief priests,
the teachers of the law and the elders mocked him.
MATTHEW 27:41

Then Herod and his soldiers ridiculed and mocked him.
LUKE 23:11

Pride

Yes, I slipped and fell on that precipice, that high place of sacrifice. I read all the books and went to every seminar of all the so-called experts. In the pride of my heart, I had some good intentions but as I was raising ordinary boys who would be extraordinary men, I wanted the glory. As my sons achieved, so did I. I forgot the One I had dedicated them to and to Whom they really belonged. He only loaned them to me for a short time. They are really His work and not mine. He gave them to me as a beautiful gift that I tried to remake in my image, which only hindered His work of conforming them to the image of His Son, Jesus Christ.

Pride goes before destruction, a haughty spirit before a fall.
PROVERBS 16:18

What is the cure for pride? Brokenness, of course. By this time, I knew God's Word, but I was and still am learning about His power.

Jesus replied, "You are in error because you do not
know the Scriptures or the power of God.
MATTHEW 22:29

...so that your faith might not rest on men's wisdom, but on God's power...
1 CORINTHIANS 2:5

I had trusted in men's wisdom and my ability, not the power of God. That is what pride really is. I found a prayer among my Twelve-Step literature that I had previously missed. I now understood more clearly what my part was.

THIRD STEP PRAYER

God, I offer myself to Thee—to build with me and to do with me as Thou wilt. Relieve me of the bondage of self, that I may better do Thy will. Take away my difficulties, that victory over them may bear witness to those I would help of Thy Power, Thy Love, and Thy Way of life. May I do Thy will always!

Shame & Guilt Versus Godly Sorrow

"Our ability to extend grace and forgiveness is directly proportional to the degree we have personally experienced it ourselves."
—**Dr. Robert McGee**

Many of us suffer needlessly from shame and guilt. I did for many years. It is a lie sent straight from Satan himself and is nothing but a tool the enemy uses to bring destruction to our lives. There is nothing about it that is good. It results in isolation, pain, fruitlessness, and despair. It keeps you in bondage, locked in that prison of hopelessness. Producing a lie he whispers over and over, "You cannot change. You are hopeless."

On the other hand, godly sorrow is sent by the Holy Spirit to bring us to repentance. Repentance leads to rededication, regeneration, renewal, restoration, and a joy-filled fruitful life. God will never expose our sin without giving us a covering in His Son. The blood of Jesus Christ is sufficient:

...who gave Himself for us, that He might redeem us from every lawless deed and purify for Himself His own special people, zealous for good works.
TITUS 2:14 (NKJV)

As it is written: "See, I lay in Zion a stone that causes men to stumble and a rock that makes them fall, and the one who trusts in him will never be put to shame.
ROMANS 9:33

Godly sorrow brings repentance that leads to salvation and leaves no regret, but worldly sorrow (shame) brings death.
2 CORINTHIANS 7:10

There is a healing balm; it is the Word of God and the Blood of Jesus. When you accept the forgiveness and healing He offers to you, then you are able to extend it to others. Time cannot heal your wounds and pain. But the Great Physician can. I know because He did it for me. But it also takes work. We must get to the root cause and get rid of it in our lives, or like a nocuous weed, it will keep coming back. But you are worth the time and effort it will take. I know because God says so:

For we know, brothers loved by God, that he has chosen you...
1 THESSALONIANS 1:4

Usefulness

It took an awful lot of years but I was finally getting to the place of willingness and full surrender. This Seventh Step Prayer was now from my heart:

My Creator, I am now willing that
you should have all of me, good and bad.
I pray that you now remove from me
every single defect of character which stands
in the way of my usefulness to you and my fellows.
Grant me strength as I go out from here to do Your bidding.

This resolve would be tested and further refined as on Thursday, March 16, 2006, my only brother died as the result of a head injury he sustained in a bicycle accident on Monday. We had secretly been planning a surprise eightieth birthday party for our mother. The ladies of Mother's church were in on the surprise and had the church decorated beautifully. But instead of a party, we had a funeral. The irony in this is even more profound, for that morning he had also gone for a ride on his motorcycle. He flew airplanes, ultra-lights, snow skied, and was a risk taker in general. Mom worried about him constantly. Afterward I asked her had she ever worried when he rode a bicycle and she said no.

Who of you by worrying can add a single hour to his life?
LUKE 12:25

The refiners' fire kept getting hotter as that same week my husband found himself unemployed from a company he had worked for twenty years.

My only brother had died, my husband was unemployed, our finances were already in bad shape because of our son's medical expenses, and our son was still ill. When I made my commitment and started praying that Seventh Step Prayer, I had no idea how much my resolve would be tested.

Though the fig tree does not bud and there are no grapes on the vines, though the olive crop fails and the fields produce no food, though there are no sheep in the pen and no cattle in the stalls,
yet I will rejoice in the LORD, I will be joyful in God my Savior.
HABAKKUK 3:17–18

Acceptance

"Nothing great was ever achieved without enthusiasm."
—**Ralph Waldo Emerson.**

Acceptance is not resignation, it is not being beaten down and lying quietly in an empty universe. It is not passivity or weakness. It is not about giving up but giving in and meeting the God of that universe in the middle of the mess with you. It is about recognizing that there is a sovereign ruler of the universe and it is not me! It is about letting go and letting God. It is about learning to trust Him in spite of your circumstances, in spite of your feelings, in spite of world conditions, in spite of what experts say. It is about a knowing that takes place within. It is an epiphany, a paradigm shift in your thinking, actions, reactions, and purpose for living each day. It is both frightening and liberating. It is motivating, yet peace filled. It is a power that can change the daily drudge into enthusiastic living.

And acceptance is the answer to all my problems today. When I am disturbed, it is because I find some person, place, thing or situation—some fact of my life—unacceptable to me, and I can find no serenity until I accept that person, place, thing, or situation as being exactly the way it is supposed to be at this moment. Nothing, absolutely nothing happens in God's world by mistake.

Until I could accept my alcoholism, I could not stay sober; unless I can accept life completely on life's terms, I cannot be happy. I need to concentrate not so much on what needs to be changed in the world as on what needs to be changed in me and in my attitudes (p. 449, *AA Big Book*).

The word enthusiasm comes from the root *en theos* meaning with God within. That is the only way we can correctly achieve acceptance. Emerson was right in his statement. Nothing great is ever achieved without God.

As surely as the truth of Christ is in me…
2 CORINTHIANS 11:10

To them God has chosen to make known among
the Gentiles the glorious riches of this mystery,
which is Christ in you, the hope of glory.
COLOSSIANS 1:27

The first step of acceptance is to accept the finished work that Christ did on the cross and then invite Him to come into your life and take over. He is not only Savior. He is Lord!

Question

While reading this, some of you may question, was she really a Christian? Yes, I was and am but a very immature and, at times, struggling one. But God takes us right where we are. He does not clean us up first or mature us first, but if we are serious about our relationship with Him, He will begin that process and keep at it. You see, my journey with Christ began with me bargaining and trying to make a conditional treaty with Him. Remember, I did not surrender because I did not want Him to tell me where to go. I would give Him parts but not the whole. I wanted Him to bless my plans for my life. I was still interested in my comfort while He was working on my character.

Joyce Meyers says once you are over your head with God, it doesn't matter how much deeper you go. But I wanted to go just deep enough that every once in a while I could get a breath, go down, touch the bottom, and come back up. I wanted control and what I thought was a security net because I was in control. God wanted me so far over my head that there was no bottom, only Him. So He did that. He moved me far from family and friends over and over. He changed my career status and path. He removed my false ability to control my children's lives. He removed my financial security. He took my only brother. He changed my plans. Now some of you are saying, why should you love and follow a God who did all this to you? Because it was ultimately for my good and for the building up of His kingdom.

Most of my life had been filled with doing good things but sometimes my motivation and purpose were wrong. I was striving to be good enough and all God wanted me to do was to surrender and let Him give me the kingdom.

"Why do you call me good?" Jesus answered.
"No one is good—except God alone."
LUKE 18:19

I know that nothing good lives in me, that is, in my sinful nature. For I have the desire to do what is good, but I cannot carry it out.
ROMANS 7:18

But I have raised you up for this very purpose, that I might show you my power and that my name might be proclaimed in all the earth.
EXODUS 9:16

I cry out to God Most High, to God, who fulfills his purpose for me.
PSALM 57:2

"Do not be afraid, little flock, for your Father has been pleased to give you the kingdom."
LUKE 12:32

The Gift

If you have hung in there and are now reading this page I want to thank you. I also want you to know that I am praying for you and this journey. I know at times it may have seemed depressing and you may have wondered, just where is this victorious Christian life I keep hearing about? The rest of this book will be just that. I will share what God replaced my high places with. When we are so busy building and worshiping at our high places, there is no time or energy left to ride the heights with Him. But as this has been a continuous lifelong process of tearing down, it has also been a continuous process of God restoring and giving. This process will not end or be complete until He calls me home to ride with Him. But the first gift He wants to give each of us is Himself, and that is done through the Holy Spirit.

"If you then, though you are evil,
know how to give good gifts to your children,
how much more will your Father in heaven
give the Holy Spirit to those who ask him!"
LUKE 11:13

For thus saith the high and lofty One that
inhabiteth eternity, whose name is Holy;
I dwell in the high and holy place, with him
also that is of a contrite and humble spirit, to
revive the spirit of the humble, and to revive the
heart of the contrite ones.

ISAIAH 57:15

Here is where the Christian road diverges from every other religious practice. All others are about people walking out their path, doing all the right things, trying to be good enough, do enough to make it to the presence of God or heaven. Only our faith teaches that in the middle of our mess, God came down to us to live in us and make a way for us.

I could not do what Jesus had already done. I just needed to accept the gift of His spirit living in and through me.

Jesus saith unto him, I am the way, the truth,
and the life: no man cometh unto the Father, but by me.

JOHN 14:6

But when the Comforter is come, whom
I will send unto you from the Father, even the Spirit of truth,
which proceedeth from the Father, he shall testify of me...

JOHN 15:26

Delight

The fondest memories I have of my children are not them winning the science fair, though they did; it is not of them making the honor roll, they did this also; or winning other numerous awards. No, my fondest memory is when they came home from school. I would give them a snack and when the weather was good let them go outside and play for an hour or so before doing their homework. I would usually go and sit and watch them play. My heart would delight at watching them and hearing the noise of their boyish and boisterous play. This is the precious memory I will keep in my heart all my life, for it is simply about delighting in them. God feels the same way about you and me.

...the LORD delights in those who fear him,
who put their hope in his unfailing love.
PSALM 147:11

He brought me out into a spacious place;
he rescued me because he delighted in me.
2 SAMUEL 22:20

For the LORD takes delight in his people;
he crowns the humble with salvation.
PSALM 149:4

"The LORD your God is with you, he is mighty to save. He will take great delight
in you, he will quiet you with his love, he will rejoice over you with singing."
ZEPHANIAH 3:17

Our Heavenly Father takes delight in each and every one of us. He created us uniquely and for His special purpose. He just delights in us, in watching us play and seeing us grow and transform into His image. We are called "human beings" not "human doings" for a reason. Yet, many of us seem to strive to do and do and do to win God's and man's approval until we are exhausted and serving Him is a burden when it should be a joy.

Is not Ephraim my dear son, the child in whom I delight?
Though I often speak against him, I still remember him.
Therefore my heart yearns for him;
I have great compassion for him," declares the LORD.
JEREMIAH 31:20

They tie up heavy loads and put them on men's shoulders, but they themselves
are not willing to lift a finger to move them.
MATTHEW 23:4

Do you feel as if you are weighed down by a heavy load? Who put it there? I can assure you that it was not your Heavenly Father. He delights in you, He yearns for a relationship with you, and He wants to delight in your play.

"For my yoke is easy and my burden is light."
MATTHEW 11:30

Koinonia

Koinonia is a Greek word that occurs about twenty times in the Bible. It is used to identify or define the ideal state of fellowship and community that should exist within the Christian church. In other words, it is godly friendships and godly fellowship. Because I love this word so much and the idealized state that it represents, I named one of my horses this many years ago while living in south Mississippi. I had decided to raise a colt from my horse, Princess. He was a perfect palomino color and had a sweet disposition. I called him Koin. From birth, he was exposed to all kinds of activity as the boys were young and they along with their friends would play in the pastures. When it was time for his training to begin for riding he was already almost bomb proof. I had a friend ride him for a month first, as I was busy working at the time. Then I brought him home and started riding him. I had only been riding him a couple of months when I took him on his first week-long trail ride to Tennessee. He did awesome and everyone was so impressed with him. On one ride, we even had a woman bucked off her horse right in front of us and she landed under his nose. He just sniffed her as if to say, are you alright?

Several months later, however, God spoke to me in a dream and told me there was a boy who needed him. I knew God wanted me to sell him to a friend who had asked me about this. I called her and told her and she said I will be down to pick him up. When she came she told me that her son, who was twelve at the time, had even been praying at school for Koin. They still own him today. I like to think that the koinonia fellowship her son had with Koin helped him navigate the difficult teen years. For that is what my horse did for me many years ago.

If you have any encouragement from being united with Christ, if any comfort from his love, if any fellowship with the Spirit, if any tenderness and compassion, then make my joy complete by being like-minded, having the same love, being one in spirit and purpose. Do nothing out of selfish ambition or vain conceit, but in humility consider others better than yourselves.
PHILIPPIANS 2:1–3

My horse submitted to me and had a gentle spirit. When we rode we were one in spirit and purpose. When I ride I feel God's pleasure and believe that this is a powerful example of what true koinonia should look like. For you see, when I am riding I can go places, do things, and accomplish what I could never do on my own. As Christ followers we are to come together in love, faith, and encouragement so that we can admonish one another and spur one another on toward love and good deeds. In unity we can accomplish far more for the kingdom. Oh and by the way, when I ride I do wear spurs and sometimes I have to use them, but with love and gentleness.

Keep You

When my boys were teens we had a few interesting events. One night a couple of brothers were spending the night with us. Our oldest son loved and was involved in the local theater and so he went to a production that evening while the other three stayed home playing video games. I went into my bedroom to read. When he came home about 11:30 he came to my bedroom to check in and asked where the other boys were. I told him they were playing video games and he replied that their car was gone. I jumped out of bed to do a house check. Their father was gone on a business trip so I was parenting alone. All three boys were gone.

Now it is past 11:30 p.m. and our town has a 12 o'clock curfew for those under 18, which they all were. Not only would the boys be taken to jail but the parents could be charged also. I called my friend who was also the mother of two sons and she came to pick me up and help me look for the boys. We had an idea of the area they would be in and as soon as we crossed the railroad tracks in the middle of town and started driving into the main neighborhood, there they were and they had a fourth friend with them from the area. They were out "rolling yards" or "TPing" them as some say with toilet paper. Now I did this myself in my teens, so don't think that I am against a little harmless teen fun. But, they had sneaked out of the house without permission and were now in violation of curfew.

When my friend picked me up I had to walk through my garage where I kept my horse equipment. I spied my long training whip and picked it up. I don't know exactly why except I had no other weapon and did not know who we might encounter at that time of night. I got out of the car and cracked that whip. I got their attention immediately. I told my son to get in the car and the others to go home. I told the brothers I had already called their father and told the other boy I would be calling his. The boys came back later and everyone apologized.

Now I did not go after my son and the other boys because I was out to get them for being bad, but to keep them from evil and from causing or having harm done to them. God feels the same way. He is not out to "GET YOU" for doing bad things but to "KEEP YOU" from evil and harm and to present you pure and spotless before His throne. I went after my son and those other boys because I love them and God does the same for us.

From this incident, I got the nickname of Psycho Mom! I think it fits.

I will search for the lost and bring back the strays.
I will bind up the injured and strengthen the weak...
EZEKIEL 34:16

Keep me from the snares they have laid for me,
from the traps set by evildoers.
PSALM 141:9

Dancing

When we moved to Slidell one of the dreams that God fulfilled was my being able to take riding lessons. I was blessed with a wonderful, gifted, and experienced trainer. Part of our lessons included dressage. I loved it and Princess excelled at it. In dressage, part of the goal is to become so much a part of your horse that the rider's signals are almost invisible. Dressage is often referred to as "dancing" with your horse. When done correctly it is an absolutely beautiful art form and expression of unity. It made me a much better rider and helped me to have a deeper understanding of our spiritual relationship with God.

David, wearing a linen ephod,
danced before the LORD with all his might...
2 SAMUEL 6:14

Let them praise his name with dancing
and make music to him with tambourine and harp.
PSALM 149:3

Remember how it was when you were a child and you would dance, run, leap, and play with joyful abandon? Have the problems and struggles of this world robbed you of that? I know there were times I just sat it out and struggled to get through. But, I came to the realization it is a choice. I choose to dance. Dancing with my horse, developing that relationship, helped me to realize that going to church and doing the right religious things do not make us right with God. Spending time alone with Him in His presence and in His Word does. Just like my trainer did for Princess and myself, we all need that special one-on-one time with our Father in training. Then, like David, we can truly dance with joyful abandon before Him. Maybe you feel as if all your dreams have been crushed to pieces and like dust blown away. Just as He gave me new dreams and even restored some of my old, he will do the same for you.

Restore to me the joy of your salvation
and grant me a willing spirit, to sustain me.
PSALM 51:12

There is a very popular song by LeeAnn Womack titled "I Hope You Dance." One of the lyrics in this song says, "when you get the choice to sit it out or dance I hope you dance."

That is what I desire for you also, my friends. May you dance and rejoice before God in this life as well as the one to come.

Singing

I sang my first solo when I was in the first grade at school. I still remember it; "How Much Is That Doggie in the Window?" I continued to sing in childrens' and adult choirs throughout most of my life. I would sometimes have a solo to sing. But I was always so insecure and would be sick at my stomach. You see, I consider myself to be just a one-talent singer. I constantly compared myself and my ability to others. My fear and my allergies also added to my problem. Yet when I am at my barn, I can sing full and open hearted, for it is to my Heavenly Father's ears and heart only.

Most of the time now, my allergies are under control. And when I sing no longer do I want to be controlled by my insecurity and fear. I want to be an instrument the Holy Spirit plays to encourage others and to please God. We do not applaud the piano or guitar when a gifted musician plays it. I do not know why I still felt compelled to sing solos in spite of my fears but I do know that helped me push through and tear down another high place in my life. Singing is important. So much so that God Himself sings over us.

"The LORD your God is with you, he is mighty to save. He will take great delight in you, he will quiet you with his love, he will rejoice over you with singing."
ZEPHANIAH 3:17

You may only be able to make a joyful noise before the Lord today but don't stop singing. For a while when my son was so ill and my heart so heavy, even singing at the barn to God and my horses was difficult, but I kept doing it. Something happens within us and within the spiritual realm when we continue to sing joyfully to our Heavenly Father. There is a quote which actually is often misquoted; "Musick has Charms to sooth a savage Breast," by William Congreve, in 'The Mourning Bride," 1697. Sometimes that savage breast is not our listeners but our own.

About midnight Paul and Silas were praying and singing hymns to God, and the other prisoners were listening to them.
ACTS 16:25

So what shall I do? I will pray with my spirit, but I will also pray with my mind; I will sing with my spirit, but I will also sing with my mind.
1 CORINTHIANS 14:15

Don't stop singing! Even when you cannot feel it in your heart, sing with your MIND! For one day, the entire Creation will join with you!

Then I heard every creature in heaven and on earth and under the earth and on the sea, and all that is in them, singing: "To him who sits on the throne and to the Lamb be praise and honor and glory and power, forever and ever!"
REVELATION 5:13

Apples

A number of years back I was watching a show on TV. They were high-lighting a special interest segment about a group of nuns. This group decided they did not want to do an anonymous prayer program any longer but wanted to get to know the individuals they were praying for. They started a prayer program called, Adopt a Nun. They would meet a couple of times a year with the people they were praying for and also correspond with each other. One sister had a couple struggling with infertility. God gave her a word for them and she wrote and told them, "Sometimes we are asking God for an apple and what He wants to give us is an orchard." *Wow*, I thought. *How many times I have begged God for the apple that hung in front of me at the time?* I would say, God look how shiny and beautiful it is. I know it has to be good for me, why won't you let me have it? But, I could not see the other side and did not know that it was wormy and rotten. And that God was trying to show me the orchard He had for me instead. But that is the way Satan works. I think of him like the wicked old witch in *Snow White*. Here my little pretty, just one bite.

A word aptly spoken is like apples of gold in settings of silver.
PROVERBS 25:11

Your plants are an orchard of pomegranates
with choice fruits, with henna and nard...
SONG OF SOLOMON 4:13

Friend, if you are struggling with God trying to get that apple today, instead listen to Him and look for the orchard He is trying to give you. There is an old saying, "You can't see the forest for the trees." Sometimes from our perspective we cannot see the orchard but trust God it is just past that group of trees in front of you.

Oh, that couple struggling with infertility, they had triplets!

Run Your Race

I never expected to be a coach in my career, but when I finished college that is what I had to do in order to have a teaching job. I was ill prepared and had to learn as I went. But, as this was the start for many in women's sports, I was not alone. The problems arose within myself as I was driven to win. I obsessed over how to develop the girls and their talents and abilities. Who to play and where to play and how many wins versus losses. I was very fortunate that as a coach I won a lot of tournament trophies, had lots of winning seasons, and even went to nationals. But I often think about the young women I had an opportunity to influence for a better life and the advancement of the kingdom of Christ. How successful was I in that area? Did I help them learn how to step out and step up?

One of the benefits that I received from this training was the skill of accessing the talents and abilities of others. It is just as important to know what we are not naturally good at as it is to know our areas of giftedness and strength. We can then do things to help develop our weak areas. I also developed a more pragmatic attitude toward myself and was able to recognize and face my own weaknesses. Before, I was insecure and defensive whenever I was criticized or questioned. I learned that a truly good leader surrounds themselves with people who are strong in their areas of weakness. I learned about strategic planning and that it is just as vital to say who you are not, as who you are. All of these were benefits that I received from doing a job I did not want to do. God had a plan. He saw my areas of weakness and He knew best how to develop me in those areas.

Maybe you are struggling today as I did then. Sometimes it is all we can do just to show up at work but I am challenging you not to just show up but to step out and step up. If you are in a difficult situation, look for what God is trying to teach you, what skills you need to learn, or maybe there is someone watching you that is learning from how you handle things that aren't easy. Maybe it is time to change careers or make a job move. These are questions for you and God to work through. But don't think that because things are difficult that God does not care. Sometimes things are most difficult when we are in the center of God's will. Long distance runners call this time of greatest difficulty "hitting the wall." But if you push through, you will win the prize.

Therefore, since we are surrounded by such a great cloud of witnesses,
let us throw off everything that hinders and the sin that so easily entangles,
and let us run with perseverance the race marked out for us.
HEBREWS 12:1

Jars of Clay

One time when the boys were in elementary school, I was at a meeting where they had a large jar stuffed with money. It was filled to the brim with bills of different denominations. The one who guessed the closest to the amount in the jar won it. I won! It was almost $300. The boys and I had lots of fun with that jar of money. We did not take it out all at once; instead whenever they needed something I would say, "go to the money jar." Eventually that jar became empty and it became the place we put our extra change, but it has never been filled again. How very different from the treasure that God promises is within each of us who receive His son into our hearts.

But we have this treasure in jars of clay to show
that this all-surpassing power is from God
and not from us.
2 CORINTHIANS 4:7

The strange paradox here is that we must first become empty of ourselves before He can fill us with the real treasure, Himself. The boys and I emptied the treasure from our jar but God first asks us to empty ourselves so He can fill us with real treasure. When we are filled with lust, greed, pride, contention, discontent, malice, rage, unforgiveness, shame, and guilt there is no room for treasure.

Where are you searching for treasure today? Are you putting your hand in an empty jar? When we are then filled with the treasures of God by the indwelling of the Holy Spirit, we can never be empty. He is our unlimited resource.

...and if you call out for insight and cry aloud
for understanding, and if you look for it as for silver
and search for it as for hidden treasure, then
you will understand the fear of the LORD
and find the knowledge of God.
PROVERBS 2:3–5

In this way they will lay up treasure for themselves
as a firm foundation for the coming age,
so that they may take hold of the life that is truly life.
1 TIMOTHY 6:19

Boys

When I was pregnant with my first son, God taught me how to love and deal with boys. Prior to that year I spent most of my time with girls, coaching was a big part of that. But that year I was also teaching Middle School Physical Education and my principal assigned me two classes of all boys. I went to him and asked why and he replied, because I know you can handle them. He gave my fellow teacher all the girls. That year I learned to love boys and how to deal with their energy and rambunctious behavior. I found out that boys are really easier to handle than girls. If they fight about something, it is usually over and they can go back to being friends. What I thought was going to be a tough year turned out to be a very fun one. God was preparing me to be the mother of two sons and a lot of strays who would come to our home over the years. I also found them to be very forgiving, especially if I included food with the confession and apology.

"…the Angel who has delivered me from all harm—may he bless these boys. May they be called by my name and the names of my fathers Abraham and Isaac, and may they increase greatly upon the earth."
GENESIS 48:16

Another thing I learned about boys was that sometimes they just cannot help but get in the middle of a mess. That is why God gave them moms. One day it had rained the night before, so I took the boys out to the track to run off some of their energy. The classroom teachers always appreciated this. Everything was fine going over to the track because I made them follow me but coming back I turned them loose and told them to line up outside the door. That was a mistake, as they proceeded to each one run ten feet off the path to jump into the middle of a rather large mud puddle and splash around before running on to line up. The clean feet I had envisioned by keeping them on the path and the right track disappeared to become a muddy mess as they followed their own choice one by one to jump in that mud. I don't know who the first culprit was but each one had a choice of which path to take. How true this is in my own life and in yours. When we try to go any other way than the one God says, we end up just like those boys, in a muddy mess.

Those boys had to face my discipline for getting off the path I directed them to follow. God does the same for us. But when we stay on His path, we are able to run in freedom!

"There are those who rebel against the light,
who do not know its ways or stay in its paths."
JOB 24:13

I run in the path of your commands,
for you have set my heart free.
PSALM 119:32

Buckner Baptist

When we lived in Dallas, I helped my friend teach GA's at church. This is a girl's mission group. It was especially fun for me since I had boys. My job was the mission activities. One day we took the girls and toured the Buckner Baptist Children's Home in Dallas. It was an amazing place but much larger than I had imagined. The dorms were several stories high and it looked like a college campus. I was very proud to see this beautiful place and to know as Baptists we had a part in providing it. But, as we toured the dorms it was evident that more people did special things for the girls than the boys. I went back to church and asked our Sunday School class if they would help us sponsor the entire group of fifteen-year-old boys. These precious people said yes. This would be one of the most fun ministries that I ever participated in. I asked their dorm parents to give me a list of needs and activities and one-by-one our class met them. We found out they only received a couple of dollars a week for snacks so we decorated a large box for each of them with their name on it and filled it with choice snacks. We took them out for pizza, had them at our home for movies and sundaes, and also to a class member's home who had remote control planes for them to fly, and a variety of other activities. I don't know who was blessed more, those boys or our class.

Religion that God our Father accepts as pure and
faultless is this: to look after orphans and widows
in their distress and to keep oneself from
being polluted by the world.
JAMES 1:27

This was in the late 1980s but since moving to Nashville, one of those boys, now a grown man, tracked us down and came to visit for a weekend. I know by his visit I received far more than I ever gave. God sent us to love on those boys and He does the same for each one of us. His promises are true and He is faithful. He will find a way to come to us when we need Him. But, we have to look with spiritual eyes for sometimes He does not look like we would expect. Sometimes He comes in the form of other people sharing His love with the hurting and broken.

I will not leave you as orphans;
I will come to you.
JOHN 14:18

Be Still

One of the hardest things for me to learn is to be still." God started teaching me this when my foot was hurt and I had to sit. But being still also can mean in our spirit. There is a fine line between knowing when to stand up and when to sit down and be silent and still. I have stood up in the past to injustice and bullies but I have also run from adversity. By nature, I do not like conflict and drama, so what is God going to do until I learn how to deal with it His way? He is going to keep on allowing me to be in the middle of it.

"The LORD will fight for you;
you need only to be still."
EXODUS 14:14

"Now then, stand still and see this great
thing the LORD is about to do before your eyes!"
1 SAMUEL 12:16

One of the first times I remember having to stand up to a bully was when I was in high school. There was a very small, thin quiet younger boy who the bigger guys would pick on. His family was very poor and they had a lot of children. I remember getting between him and his aggressors one day and giving them a piece of my mind. He was left alone at least on the bus when I was present from then on. But years later after I was out of college, I learned he had committed suicide. I was convicted that I had not gone far enough to help this young man. How different his life might have been if we had visited his family and included them within our circle of friendship. This was a time I should not have been still.

Being still does not mean we never do anything. It is not a Pollyanna attitude, nor does it absolve us of responsibility. It means that we learn to do our part and then wait on God to do His.

Therefore put on the full armor of God,
so that when the day of evil comes,
you may be able to stand your ground,
and after you have done everything, to stand.
EPHESIANS 6:13

In those days, I did not know about or understand the armor of God, so I was not fully dressed or prepared for battle. We cannot be still enough in spirit to stand quietly waiting on God without it.

$\mathcal{D}$ressed

I was not able to take swimming lessons as a child but the summer between my junior and senior years of high school, I taught myself. I was a very weak and unskilled swimmer when I entered college but determined to improve. I took Intermediate Swimming first to learn the proper strokes, and to develop my strength and endurance. Then I took Advanced Swimming, Lifesaving, and finally my Water Safety Instructors certification course. I was never a great swimmer but determined to be the best that I could. Our Lifesaving class instructor was a male and also one of my bosses as I worked as a Secretary for the Physical Education Department. One day in class he was having us dive in at the deep end and swim the length of the pool. I was wearing a two-piece suit. I dove in like the rest of the class but when I broke the surface of the water realized I had lost my top. I was not dressed properly for this job and suffered the consequences of humiliation. We all laughed and I am sure this story has been shared many times since by my instructor and fellow classmates. But I went out and purchased a one-piece suit so that I would be dressed correctly for that activity from then on. Just as I needed to be dressed correctly for swimming, we need to be dressed correctly in order to serve Jesus Christ by serving others.

Therefore, as God's chosen people, holy and dearly loved, clothe yourselves
with compassion, kindness, humility, gentleness and patience...
COLOSSIANS 3:12

Because I prepared myself, I later was able to work as a lifeguard and swim instructor over the summers, even when I was a teacher. Not only had I prepared myself outwardly by buying a one-piece swimsuit but I had done the hard work of training for this job and learning from the right instructors. This is also true in our spiritual lives. We must be dressed, prepared, and ready to be used of God.

The Armor of God

Finally, be strong in the Lord and in his mighty power.
Put on the full armor of God so that you can take
your stand against the devil's schemes.
For our struggle is not against flesh and blood,
but against the rulers, against the authorities,
against the powers of this dark world and against
the spiritual forces of evil in the heavenly realms.
Therefore put on the full armor of God,
so that when the day of evil comes,
you may be able to stand your ground, and
after you have done everything, to stand.
Stand firm then, with the belt of truth buckled
around your waist, with the breastplate of
righteousness in place, and with your feet fitted
with the readiness that comes from the gospel of peace.

In addition to all this, take up the shield of faith,
with which you can extinguish all the
flaming arrows of the evil one.
Take the helmet of salvation and the sword of the Spirit,
which is the word of God.
And pray in the Spirit on all occasions with
all kinds of prayers and requests.
With this in mind, be alert and always keep on
praying for all the saints.
EPHESIANS 6:10–18

Stand

We can never stand until we have first learned to be still. Otherwise we just turn and run every time adversity comes. We also cannot stand without first being prepared. But for the Christ follower, this is not an option. He is our commander in chief and He has given us our orders.

> *"Get yourself ready! Stand up and say to them whatever I command you. Do not be terrified by them, or I will terrify you before them."*
> JEREMIAH 1:17

How do we get ready? One of the ways is what you are doing now: read, study, and learn from others. Find a good Bible teaching, Bible believing, love-filled church, join up, and show up regularly. Read the Word of God yourself and spend time meditating on it and in prayer with Him. Ask God to send the Holy Spirit the Teacher to you. I promise He will. Then do not just sit, soak, and sour, but stand up for Jesus Christ and do what He commands you to.

The Greatest Commandment

One of the teachers of the law came and heard them debating.
Noticing that Jesus had given them a good answer, he asked him,
"Of all the commandments, which is the most important?"
"The most important one," answered Jesus, "is this:
'Hear, O Israel, the Lord our God, the Lord is one.
Love the Lord your God with all your heart and
with all your soul and with all your mind and with all your
strength.' The second is this: 'Love your neighbor as yourself.'
There is no commandment greater than these."
"Well said, teacher," the man replied.
"You are right in saying that
God is one and there is no other but him.
To love him with all your heart, with all your understanding and
with all your strength, and to love your neighbor as yourself is
more important than all burnt offerings and sacrifices."
When Jesus saw that he had answered wisely, he said to him,
"You are not far from the kingdom of God."
And from then on no one dared ask him any more questions.

MARK 12:28–34

Yes, my dear reader and friend, the most important thing we must dress ourselves in is LOVE! Without it, we are naked and unprepared, hopeless to stand.

Hairy Chins

This probably seems like a strange topic to address to some of you but God is always teaching me in strange ways. A friend of mine and I were talking the other day about how now that we are in menopause, things are changing. One is that strange stray hairs appear on our chins or neck area. Sometimes we do not see them because another thing is happening our vision is getting weaker also. She was sharing how a friend was talking with her and thought she had a loose long hair on her chin and was embarrassed when she went to pick it off and found out it was attached. God must love watching us deal with these issues. I am convinced it is because He wants us to stop taking ourselves and outward appearances so seriously. The wonderful part of this process is not only do I not see my own faults, I do not see those of others. Maybe God gives us these foggy lenses so that we can begin to really see ourselves and others.

So we fix our eyes not on what is seen, but on what is unseen.
For what is seen is temporary, but what is unseen is eternal.
2 CORINTHIANS 4:18

I counsel you to buy from me gold refined in the fire,
so you can become rich; and white clothes to wear,
so you can cover your shameful nakedness;
and salve to put on your eyes, so you can see.
REVELATION 3:18

It is almost as if God is putting that salve on my eyes so that I can see past the superficial decaying body to the eternal spirit within people. He is teaching me to love them as Jesus loved the church. He is teaching me to love myself also. This is not an easy process because it requires dying.

Then he turned to his disciples and said privately,
"Blessed are the eyes that see what you see."
LUKE 10:23

Goats and Kids

There were five of us grandchildren that grew up together. The oldest was my cousin, he was three years my senior, and the rest of us followed his lead. We also had a variety of animals in our life and goats were a big part in those years. Our grandfather owned a billy (male) goat with large curved horns. My cousin and brother played with him and taught him to chase them and try to butt them. Our grandfather did not know about this game. One day granddaddy was tying the goat along a fence line to eat the vegetation growing on it. He bent over to untie the rope and move it further down and his backside presented a perfect target. The billy hit him and he somersaulted over the fence. We five children were watching and enjoyed a tremendous laugh. Granddaddy was unhurt and he got up laughing also. I don't think we ever told him that the boys had trained the goat to do that. As children, we all do things that seem to be nothing but great fun, a game, but can end up harming someone else or placing them in danger. What we think is just harmless mischief can actually be injurious to ourselves or others.

When I was a child, I spake as a child,
I understood as a child, I thought as a child:
but when I became a man, I put away childish things.
1 CORINTHIANS 13:11 (KJV)

It is time for many of us to grow up in Christ. What habits have we developed or activities involved in that are really harmful to ourselves or others? Who is following our example just as we followed my cousin's? I am not speaking about genuine fun. God, as I already shared, delights in our laughter and enjoyment of all He has created for us. Our goat play was just innocent childish fun. I am speaking about unhealthy behavior that shortens our lives and causes harm.

You may think what you are doing is your secret, but just like the goat butting my grandfather, secrets have a way of revealing themselves at awkward times.

Brothers, stop thinking like children.
In regard to evil be infants,
but in your thinking be adults.
1 CORINTHIANS 14:20

Out of the Boat

The story of Jesus walking on the water and Peter getting out of the boat and walking toward Him has always been one of my favorites. Not because of Peter, but because of the other eleven disciples cowering in the bottom of the boat in fear. For years I have studied and meditated upon this passage and prayed to God for wisdom to learn from it. As Peter was throwing his leg over the side of the boat, I am sure the others were trying to pull him back in. They were calling and telling him not to climb out. Not because they feared for him but for themselves. They yelled, "You will turn the boat over!"

When I first began struggling with the issues within our organized church and did not want to "play church" anymore but wanted to learn and "become the church," this is what happened to me and still happens today. The eleven disciples in the bottom of the boat were still His disciples but they missed the blessing Peter received because of fear and lack of faith. I have climbed out of the boat and like Peter, I have walked on the water, spiritually. I have even began to sink at times because I took my eyes off of Jesus and looked at the waves around and listened to the voices back in the bottom of the boat calling to me. But once I got out of the bottom of the boat and started walking toward Jesus, I found a whole lot of other people were out there doing the same.

"Come," he said. Then Peter got down out of the boat,
walked on the water and came toward Jesus.
MATTHEW 14:29

The time is short and many are suffering. It is time to stop just going to church and become the church. Now I don't mean that literally we do not gather as a church for worship, instruction, and fellowship, but that is not enough. The church is not the building in which we gather, WE **are the church,** the very Bride of Christ. Don't be satisfied to cower in the bottom of the church boat and don't settle for less than all God has for you. Throw your leg over the side and climb out today. But make sure you keep your eyes on Jesus.

Immediately Jesus reached out his hand and caught him.
"You of little faith," he said, "why did you doubt?"
And when they climbed into the boat, the wind died down.
Then those who were in the boat worshiped him, saying,
"Truly you are the Son of God."
MATTHEW 14:31–33

What are the benefits of this? Not only will you walk on the water of faith toward Jesus but even those in the boat will believe and then Jesus will come into the boat with you.

Follow Christ

I do not consider myself a horse trainer but I have taken several young horses and made excellent trail partners of them. The first thing I do is make sure they have a good mind. No matter how much you work with a horse, you cannot change some things. Then I get a friend with an older, very dependable, and experienced trail horse to ride in front so we can follow. My younger horse then learns not only from the experience of being on the trail and from me, but from the horse he is following also. I have also taken my horse many times and done this for other friends starting a new horse on the trail. We do this alone at first and not in a group.

Also the horse has already been receiving training under the saddle prior to going on the trail. In other words, you don't throw a saddle on a young horse for the first time and take him right out on the trail. Training is progressive. I used to encourage the youth I taught to witness to their friends and bring them to our church activities. But I told them not to go into questionable activities or places in the world.

In the prior post, I talked about getting out of the boat but if we get out to soon and are not prepared, we will sink. Just as I would not take a young horse on the trail without preparing him first, we also need to be prepared in order to follow Christ wherever He may lead. Many churches do an excellent job of teaching and training, but others fall short. They may be good about getting people saved but are not preparing them to navigate the world we must live in effectively for Christ. My horses have to learn to navigate steep hills, cross rivers, get around or over large rocky areas, fallen trees, and other trail hazards. They have to learn not to panic in dangerous situations or when presented with unexpected events. They have to learn to trust me—their rider and guide.

But in your hearts set apart Christ as Lord.
Always be prepared to give an answer to everyone
who asks you to give the reason for the hope that
you have. But do this with gentleness and respect...
1 PETER 3:15

Before we get out of the boat, we must first learn to trust our rider and guide, Jesus Christ. We must learn His character and know His voice. Jesus said He was sending His disciples out as sheep among wolves. He also told us to be as wise as a serpent but as harmless as a dove. These are hard teachings and before getting out of the boat we must learn many things. Then Jesus did something else; He sent them out in pairs, He did not send them out alone.

After this the Lord appointed seventy-two others and sent them two by two
ahead of him to every town and place where he was about to go.
LUKE 10:1

Feed My Sheep

They weren't sheep but about forty head of large ponies that my dad and granddad had bought in Oklahoma that I helped feed one winter. The original owner had had a heart attak and could no longer care for them. I was given the task, which I loved, of feeding them every day. Many of them were wild also so I made gentling a part of my daily task. I was feeding them more than just their daily meal, I was teaching them about how to relate to humans. That is what Jesus meant when He told Peter to feed His sheep. He didn't just mean our daily bread or meals but His Word. He wants us to learn of Him and how to live this life for and with Him.

The third time he said to him, "Simon son of John, do you love me?" Peter was hurt because Jesus asked him the third time, "Do you love me?" He said, "Lord, you know all things; you know that I love you." Jesus said, "Feed my sheep.
JOHN 21:17

Jesus expects us to grow. He does not want us to just get saved and stay safely in the pen but He expects us to grow as Christ followers and then to lead more to become Christ followers. We are learning more and more about nutrition and how important the right foods are for us to be healthy.

The same is true for us to grow as followers of Christ. We must feast upon His written Word and then learn to feast in the presence of the "Living" Word by prayer and meditation. When we meditate upon the Word of God in quietness and solitude, the Holy Spirit will come.

What if a baby were never given solid food but was expected to live and grow into a mature adult on mush? It is time for many of us to start feasting upon the table that Christ has set before us. It is time for the church to grow up in Him.

But solid food is for the mature, who by constant use have trained themselves to distinguish good from evil.
HEBREWS 5:14

Growing up can be very scary because of the increase in responsibility we receive. I was in about the sixth grade when I fed those horses all winter. But that responsibility helped me to grow and mature and be able to handle more. Maybe that is one of the reasons you have stopped growing in Christ, fear of an increase in responsibility. If you have stopped growing you are just sitting, soaking, and maybe souring. God meant for us to be useful and to be used to feed others. However, if we are souring, we are not very tasty. But just as sour milk can be used to make buttermilk, God can change us and make us more tasty and useful also.

Buttermilk

Originally, buttermilk was the liquid left over from churning butter from cream. Before cream could be skimmed from whole milk, it was left to sit for a period of time to allow the cream and milk to separate. During this time, the milk would be fermented by the naturally occurring lactic acid-producing bacteria in the milk. This acidic environment also helps prevent potentially harmful microorganisms from growing, increasing shelf-life. In other words, buttermilk is very healthy for us. In fact, when I was a small child I became very ill and the only thing my mother could give me was buttermilk.

It actually saved my life. Buttermilk has been shown to have many health benefits; it is lower in fat than regular milk, high in potassium, vitamin B12, calcium, riboflavin, and is a good source of phosphorus. It is also more easily and quickly digested than regular milk and that is probably why my doctor had me drink it when I was ill. This may be interesting but what does it have to do with following Christ, you are probably asking? Several things: first the milk had to sit in a warm place for a while. We need to participate in and be committed to a Christ honoring, Bible believing and teaching church. It is there where the work usually begins to separate us from the things of the world and teach us the things of Christ. It had to have time to ferment and for healthy bacteria to grow. Just as we need time to grow in Christ. Another benefit is that these bacteria increase shelf-life, which is interesting since we are to share with others both how to have and experience real life now, and also how to have eternal life with Christ. Also, buttermilk is healthy in itself and for others. God desires for us to be healthy physically, mentally, socially, and spiritually.

...and when he found him, he brought him to Antioch.
So for a whole year Barnabas and Saul met with the church
and taught great numbers of people.
The disciples were called Christians first at Antioch.
ACTS 11:26

On the next Sabbath almost the whole
city gathered to hear the word of the Lord.
ACTS 13:44

The word of the Lord spread through the whole region.
ACTS 13:49

We must be growing in our walk with Christ and when we are, it is contagious and progressive. It cannot be contained but will spread to others. If you have been one of those just sitting, soaking, and souring, remember God wants you to be healthy and useful. He wants you to become BUTTERMILK.

No Strangers

Until I was sixteen, my grandfather and father had a general merchandise store in what is now Pelham, Alabama, just south of Birmingham. It was the largest store in the area. This was before the time of large super markets. We would go to the farm for weekends and longer summer trips only.

When I was born, my parents had a small apartment in the back of the store. As I grew old enough to stand holding onto something, my mother would open the connecting door, put the baby gate up, and let me stand watching my father and other people in the store. People would do as they always do with a baby and come over to talk with me and fuss over me. In this way, I learned to love people and to realize that a stranger was just a friend I had not met yet. Also, since a wide variety of people came into the store, I did not develop prejudices against people because of color or the way they dressed. I just found them interesting and different.

Eventually we moved into a small house next door to the store but by then I could run back and forth to visit my father and grandfather and talk with the customers. But times change and the big super markets came into popularity. My grandfather was ready to retire and so he sold the store and we all moved to our farms. My dad started a new business as a livestock dealer. That first year was rough and he had to work nights at the cotton gin but his hard work paid off and he developed a successful business. The move to our farm was good for us. It came at just the right time in my teen years also.

Dear friend, you are faithful in what you are doing for the brothers,
even though they are strangers to you.
3 JOHN 1:5

I developed strong life-long friendships with the people there, especially at Walter Baptist Church. My mother still attends church there today. The people loved me through those years and beyond and put up with my teenage antics and mischief. Their spiritual support helped me on my journey of healing and ministry. I have learned that strangers are sometimes brothers and sisters that God wants to bring together for His purpose.

There is nowhere I can go that God has not been first, and He has brothers and sisters waiting for me there.

Peter, an apostle of Jesus Christ, To God's elect, strangers in the world, scattered throughout Pontus, Galatia, Cappadocia, Asia and Bithynia...
1 PETER 1:1

Mother's Love

When we moved to our farm, my mother also had to go to work. Her first job was working at a sewing factory. She would go and have to sit and sew all day long. She would come home at night exhausted. As I shared that first year was very tight financially, more than even my parents let my brother and I know. They knew Christmas would be very lean. After I had gone to bed at night, Mother would stay up sewing. I did not know this. I thought she was in bed also, as the machine was in her bedroom. When Christmas came she presented me with a beautiful new dress that she had been staying up at night making for me. I have received many beautiful and expensive gifts through the years, but none I have treasured as this. Even later, as they prospered, she and I developed a Christmas tradition of going shopping the day after Christmas to buy many new dresses. But none have I valued or remembered as that one made of sacrifice. And through the years, whenever I would get upset with her about something, I have always kept this in my heart to pull out and put things in perspective.

"'Each of you must respect his mother and father,
and you must observe my Sabbaths.
I am the LORD your God.'"
LEVITICUS 19:3

155

Her children arise and call her blessed;
her husband also, and he praises her…
PROVERBS 31:28

As long as I live and now hopefully generations to come will share this story of loving sacrifice in honor of my mother. She was later able to get a position at the local hospital in dietary until she retired. She loved that job and it perfectly suited her.

Recreation

I have been blessed to have many wonderful times of recreation. When I taught Physical Education I would tell people "my work is your play." Our culture has somehow made play a negative concept but nothing could be further from the truth. It is not just that "all work and no play makes Jack a dull boy" but it makes him sad, sick, and miserable also. God designed us to play or have times of recreation. The root of recreation is recreate. It is an absolute necessity for us to have times where we draw away from our high-tech and high-pace society. We must unplug from technology and plug into creation to reconnect with our creator. He is the source of true creativity.

One of our favorite vacations was spent camping in the west. We traced the Anasazi tribe from their last known residence in the Grand Canyon, back across the Colorado River and to Mesa Verde, their largest known habitation. It truly was a special trip and memory for all of us and it was good for us physically, mentally, and spiritually.

The Bible tells us that Jesus regularly pulled away from the crowds and population areas to go to the wilderness and be alone with His Father. Instead of making some big expensive vacation destination resort your pick this year, I encourage you to go to the wilderness.

And he withdrew himself into the wilderness, and prayed.
LUKE 5:16

The wilderness and the solitary place shall be glad for them;
and the desert shall rejoice, and blossom as the rose.
ISAIAH 35:1

And in the morning, rising up a great while before day,
he went out, and departed into a solitary place, and there prayed.
MARK 1:35

Maybe instead of coming home stressed from the schedule and money you spent, you just might return refreshed, refueled, and, in fact, re-created. He is waiting for you to come and spend time alone with Him.

The earth is filled with your love, O LORD; teach me your decrees.
PSALM 119:64

A Living or A Life

As I write this book, we are in the middle of the worst economic time since the great depression. But also at no time in history have we had more things and yet less time to enjoy. Families are pulled apart and separated by many miles. With work schedules, sports, school, and extra-curricular activities, people are busy but are they having a real joy-filled life or is it just a filled life? Is it all about competition or being complete in Christ? About being healthy or about being made whole? You may be doing a lot of good things but are you taking the time for the best? There are a record number of foreclosures, bankruptcies, and unemployment. Those who are working are working longer hours for less pay. Yet we are still consumed by consumerism, getting more and more stuff, so the economy can keep chugging along. There is also an epidemic of alcohol and drug abuse, children in single parent homes, mental illness, violence, and homelessness. It can be a very frightening thing to take a leap of faith and jump off this train but the results are worth it. I know because I have done it.

This was part of my high places that had to be torn down. But now that I ride the heights with Him, I never want to go back to the old way my way of trying to do life. I know we all have to make a living and sometimes we are stuck in a very difficult job and circumstances. But do not let the expectations of this culture place burdens upon you and your family that God does not intend for you to carry.

One thing we did to simplify was to cut down on Christmas giving. I told the children the wise men only brought Jesus three gifts, so that was all they would get. I wanted to try and help my children get off this path of greed. In the end, it is all just stuff. I wanted my children to see that we love and value people and just use stuff, not the other way around.

I know how difficult this is when you are in the midst of raising a family. But it is also the right time to help them develop habits that will help them build a life as well as make a living. The Bible tells us about a man who loved his stuff but not people.

"Then he said, 'This is what I'll do. I will tear down
my barns and build bigger ones, and there I will store
all my grain and my goods. "But God said to him,
'You fool! This very night your life will be demanded from you.
Then who will get what you have prepared for yourself?'
"This is how it will be with anyone who stores
up things for himself but is not rich toward God."
LUKE 12:18–21

Maybe you cannot identify with this right now because it is all you can do to just survive and pay your bills, but you can still be storing up riches for yourself in Christ. In fact, if you are prayerfully reading this book, that is just what you are doing.

Overcoming

I think it is impossible to ride the heights and to have an abundant whole life without first overcoming unbelief. I have struggled at times with believing and trusting God. Why did God not answer my prayer for my father to stop drinking? Why did God not make my life easy, neat, and safe? Why was I not given health, wealth, and popularity? Why did God not answer my prayers my way? I know what is best for my life, right?

When things are difficult we don't understand why evil seems to flourish and good people suffer. If we look around, we will lose hope because the world seems hopeless. Why should we struggle to do the right thing when so many prosper who do evil? When I was younger, I struggled with these and more questions. But, I made up my mind to believe God and take Him at His Word. In other words, I read and studied the Bible and began to look there for answers. God could have made us all compliant but then there would be no free will, no choice. I then started reading and learning about the lives of other Christians. How God helped them through difficult times, answered prayer sometimes in unexpected ways, and sometimes gave them a miracle. I did not overcome unbelief all at once, but slowly over time as I got to know God and saw Him work in my life and answer prayer His way, not mine.

Immediately the boy's father exclaimed,
"I do believe; help me overcome my unbelief!"
MARK 9:24

They overcame him by the blood of the Lamb
and by the word of their testimony…
REVELATION 12:11

Many churches are good at giving people the blood of the Lamb but fail to allow others to share the word of their testimony. Yet that is how we overcome unbelief. I love to read about and listen to others share the great and wonderful things that God has done in and through their lives.

That is the main reason I am writing this book, to encourage you on your journey home to God. Maybe you are a believer and just picked this book out of curiosity. Maybe you are in a time of struggle and need hope. Maybe you are disillusioned and have been hurt by others in the church. Maybe you are a seeker trying to figure out if this God/Jesus thing is for real. Whatever reason you thought you are reading this book for, I can tell you it is not by chance. I have prayed for you, dear reader, and this is a God appointment. He is ready for you to become an **overcomer** also.

Learning to Trust

The boys were born in the town of Temple, Texas. I loved it there but it was a long way from my home and family. So when the oldest was two years old and the youngest two months old, my husband took a new job in Houston. When you ask God for more faith to help you overcome unbelief, guess what you will get? Opportunities to practice faith.

Joe moved to Houston leaving me at home alone with two small children to sell our home. This was in 1984, and the real estate market was terrible in Texas. After several months of our home not selling, we moved into a rental in Houston. But a man contacted Joe with an opportunity in New Orleans promising him if he did well there, in two years he could open an office in Montgomery, Alabama. So after nine months in Houston and our home not selling in Temple, we moved to New Orleans for the first time.

We rented a home there in Metarie. We moved there the first of May and six months later, the last of October, the owner laid Joe off. He had gotten him through the busy months of summer. Our home in Temple still had not sold. That next week Joe's Regional Manager from his old company contacted him about a position in Dallas. We did not even have to search for a job or go without a paycheck. So we moved to the northwest side of Dallas and rented a home there.

Within a few months, Joe's boss left that company for another in Dallas. I told Joe that I believed he would call him when he had a good opportunity and he did. Joe accepted that position but the office was in the far southeast part of the Dallas metro area. So we had to move again, this time to the suburb of Allen. There we leased a home with the option to purchase as soon as our home in Temple sold. A few months after moving into this home and paying our rent on time each month, we were informed that the house was being foreclosed on and that we could not purchase it, but had to move again.

Our home in Temple sold. We found a much better home in a better and more established neighborhood that we loved and we were able to live there for five years. This time of moving and our home not selling was two years. We had to pay the house payment, plus rent, moving expenses, and care for ourselves and children, and yet in all that time we never had a bill that was late. We would get down to as little as $15 in the checking account and the next payday would be several days away but we never had a need that was not met. Mysterious checks would come in the mail—old refunds or rebates. God used this time of testing to help me develop my faith and trusting muscle.

God takes us right where we are even with just a little faith and a lot of unbelief.

"Have faith in God," Jesus answered.
MARK 11:22

If that is how God clothes the grass of the field,
which is here today, and tomorrow is thrown into the fire,
how much more will he clothe you, O you of little faith!
LUKE 12:28

Barefootin'

"Earth's crammed with heaven, and every common bush afire with God.
And only he who sees takes off his shoes, the rest sit round and pluck blackberries."
—Elizabeth Barrett Browning

When I was a child, most of the summer I ran around barefoot. I could run this way through the fields, on roads, everywhere. There was a special freedom in this that I no longer have. My feet are too tender to hardly walk on my driveway, let alone run through a field. Yet there is something akin to holiness we have by having direct contact with the earth this way. God even sometimes requires it of us. Is it for humility or some other purpose?

"Do not come any closer," God said.
"Take off your sandals, for the place where
you are standing is holy ground."
EXODUS 3:5

"Then the Lord said to him,
'Take off your sandals; the place where
you are standing is holy ground."
ACTS 7:33

One Sunday many years ago, I was sitting on the front pew of our church waiting to sing a solo. This was the first Sunday of a special week of Prayer. The voice of the Holy Spirit spoke to me and said, "Take off your shoes for today you are on Holy Ground." I did not want to do this. The church was a very big formal church and I was very unsure how they would view this and told God so. But, He said again, "Take your shoes off while you sing." So I did and told the congregation why. I know some did not approve and some thought I was crazy, but some understood. This was yet another way of God teaching me to please Him and not to seek to please people. His Word tells us that when two or more are gathered in His name, He is present and part of the Holy Communion we have with Him in Prayer. Yet why do we take it so much for granted and spend so little time in prayer while in church? Is it because in our culture we want to be entertained every minute? Can we not quiet our minds and hearts to watch and pray with Him just one hour?

Throughout time, there have been those who had eyes to see and hearts that cried out to the Creator of this Universe. When we come to recognize the supreme authority and holiness of our God, we, too, will take our shoes off in awe and reverence and learn to watch for others who are going barefoot also.

Prayer

What is this thing called prayer that we talk about so much but tend to do so little of? In the denomination I grew up in and am still a member of, our Wednesday night services are called Prayer Meeting. Yet only about five to ten minutes at the most is usually spent in prayer. When I ask why this is so, I get a mixed bag of answers. Is it that even pastors have a problem, just as the disciples did, with spending just one hour in prayer? Is it a lack of control a fear of what might happen? Jesus had some very specific instructions for us regarding this.

And as he taught them, he said, "Is it not written:
"'My house will be called a house of prayer for all nations'?
But you have made it 'a den of robbers.'"
MARK 11:17

...these I will bring to my holy mountain
and give them joy in my house of prayer.
ISAIAH 56:7

I am reminded of what Jim Cybala relates in the growth of his church, The Brooklyn Tabernacle. He gives full credit to the people praying together.

He has shared that they only experienced this phenomenal growth and watched amazing life transformations after becoming a true house of prayer.

Then he returned to his disciples and found them sleeping.
"Could you men not keep watch with me for one hour?" he asked Peter.
MATTHEW 26:40

In this scripture, Jesus is referring to praying together in the garden before His crucifixion. What did He mean though by the phrase, "keep watch"? Does this have a special significance for us today in the importance of praying together for others?

It's like a man going away:
He leaves his house and puts his servants in charge,
each with his assigned task, and tells the
one at the door to keep watch.
MARK 13:34

Could God be telling us that only in prayer are we able to defend ourselves and His church? Is the church losing its power and experiencing such turmoil because it is failing in this directive? It is clear that this is His first and greatest assignment to us. Are we to be the guards at the door keeping the enemy out of God's house? Without prayer, we just may become the enemy.

Getting Started

I remember well when I first made the decision to get serious about my prayer life. I was going to take the Bible literally and follow it exactly. The King James translation said I was to go into my closet and pray in secret and that is what I would do.

But thou, when thou prayest, enter into thy closet,
and when thou hast shut thy door,
pray to thy Father which is in secret;
and thy Father which seeth in secret shall reward thee openly.
MATTHEW 6:6

The boys were still in pre-school and that first morning as soon as Joe left for work, I got up to start my time of prayer. I went into our closet, turned off the light, and knelt down in prayer. After a moment, the closet door opened and there stood my precious husband, looking down at me in a dark closet in shock. I am sure he wondered if he should leave me home alone that day with the boys. I have spent many precious hours since alone in prayer with our Heavenly Father. He truly has taught me how to watch and pray for an hour or however long is needed. I have seen Him work to change me and to answer my prayers in many different ways. Sometimes though I simply have been struggling and did not know what or how to pray about something. He has been there in and through those times also.

In the same way, the Spirit helps us in our weakness.
We do not know what we ought to pray for,
but the Spirit himself intercedes for us with groans
that words cannot express.
ROMANS 8:26

While sometimes Jesus did go alone to a solitary place to pray, I have found that the greatest results have come when I prayed in unity with others.

These all continued with one accord in prayer
and supplication, with the women,
and Mary the mother of Jesus, and with his brethren.
ACTS 1:14

And when the day of Pentecost was fully come,
they were all with one accord in one place.
ACTS 2:1

In Acts 2, the people are given the Holy Spirit, but you have to go back and read what comes before in Acts 1 to understand why. They were praying together! Praying together creates unity! The power of God will come when we pray together in one accord or unity as Jesus instructed us to do in His model prayer. Not our own agenda but "thy kingdom come thy will be done."

By Prayer

When my youngest son became ill, I rushed him to the hospital but I also started calling prayer warriors that I knew. I am blessed to have people within my friend circle that are dedicated in praying for others. Did he achieve the level of wellness that he has by medical care or by prayer? I believe it was a combination of both.

"Again, I tell you that if two of you on earth agree
about anything you ask for, it will be done for you
by my Father in heaven. For where two or
three come together in my name, there am I with them."
MATTHEW 18:19–20

My son's healing has been an encouragement to his doctors. I love telling them about all the prayer that has gone up to heaven on his behalf. We even had a friend come and help us anoint him with oil and have a special time of prayer for him.

He replied, "This kind can come out only by prayer. "
MARK 9:29

Jesus himself said that some things can only be accomplished by prayer. Do not take it lightly when someone tells you I am praying for you. That may very well be the greatest thing they can do for you. I would rather someone regularly and fervently pray for me and the ministry God has given me than to just give a monetary donation. While the money will help in the short term, the prayers have eternal and lasting results. Are you having trouble just getting started praying? Then take the example that Jesus gave and start there.

Jesus' Teaching on Prayer

One day Jesus was praying in a certain place.
When he finished, one of his disciples said to him,
"Lord, teach us to pray, just as John taught his disciples."
LUKE 11:1

"This, then, is how you should pray:
Our Father which art in heaven, Hallowed be thy name. Thy kingdom come, Thy will be done in earth, as it is in heaven. Give us this day our daily bread. And forgive us our debts, as we forgive our debtors. And lead us not into temptation, but deliver us from evil: For thine is the kingdom, and the power, and the glory, forever. Amen."
MATTHEW 6:9–13

By My Spirit

Perhaps the least understood of the Trinity is the Holy Spirit. I know in the denomination of which I practice, He is the one most feared. We call on Him and sing to Him but experiencing Him and His control over our lives is something else.

When my dad was killed, everything fell on my shoulders. My mother and brother were too broken to even be much help planning the funeral. Early that first morning I was home, before I started the day's work, I went on the front porch and prayed. I told my Heavenly Father that I really needed special help to do all that had to be done and then I sat in silence waiting. The Holy Spirit came to me then in quietness, strength, and power. It was the most amazing feeling I have ever had. It sustained me through the weeks and years of work that were ahead. My father had not left a will and my grandfather had died just six weeks prior and his estate had not been settled yet. So after the funeral was over, my work would really begin.

So he said to me, "This is the word of the LORD to Zerubbabel:
'Not by might nor by power, but by my Spirit,' says the LORD Almighty."
ZECHARIAH 4:6

I think so many are afraid of letting go of their control and submitting to the control of the Holy Spirit for fear of what God will require of them. They might be made laughing stocks; many of His prophets were. He might take away everything they have, like Job. He might ask them to go to another nation or to strange people, like Jonah. He might make their neat, organized, comfortable, and short worship experience at church chaotic, long, and uncomfortable like in Acts 2.

I have had the same fears. I now know the difference between worshipping and acting in my spirit and worshipping and living in His. I prefer the Holy Spirit living and working in and through my life.

Then the Spirit of the LORD came upon him in power.
JUDGES 14:19

The Spirit of the LORD will come upon you in power,
and you will prophesy with them;
and you will be changed into a different person.
1 SAMUEL 10:6

I tried very hard for many years to change and tear down the high places in my life but it was only after I surrendered to the Holy Spirit and allowed Him to live and work in and through my life did the healing change come.

The Spirit's Fire

When my oldest son graduated from high school, we had an awards night. I was and am very proud of him not just for his accomplishments but for his character and who he is as a person. But that night I blew it! I was a disciplinarian in our family but also practiced a lot of positive motivation but that night for some unknown reason, all of that was lost to me. When his name and GPA was announced, he missed the highest honors by a fraction of a point. I was stressing over his leaving home and how we were going to pay his college bills but also I wanted him to achieve more in life than I or his Father had. I pushed him to be his best and sometimes maybe too hard. But that night I am ashamed to say I really quenched his spirit.

When we were leaving I impulsively stated something about if only he had worked a little harder he would have been in the top. Immediately I was pricked in my spirit and apologized to him. But it was too late; I had already crushed his spirit for he was thinking the same thing. I have talked with him about this several times since and he has forgiven me but I find it hard to forgive myself.

My Father had done the very same thing to me and I had vowed never to do that to my children. One day I had come to show him my report card. I had all A's except for one B. He said nothing about the A's but pointed to the B and asked why it was there. A careless word, a thoughtless action, how easily we wound each other and quench the spirit. One definition of quench is to put out or extinguish; to suppress or squelch.

Do not put out the Spirit's fire...
1 THESSALONIANS 5:19

How do we find a remedy for this? By doing as I did and immediately ask for forgiveness and seeking ways to make amends. And also by asking God to give us His Holy Spirit to live in and through us. Without Him it is impossible to live this life in a way that pleases Him and blesses others.

The Spirit of the LORD will rest on him—
the Spirit of wisdom and of understanding,
the Spirit of counsel and of power,
the Spirit of knowledge and of the fear of the LORD...
ISAIAH 11:2

How do we quench the Holy Spirit's fire in our lives? I believe it is by rejection and disobedience. When we are operating in the flesh and out of fear we will do and say things that grieve the Spirit of God and put out that fire within ourselves and others. It is like taking a bucket of water and pouring it over a small fire. Before it can be relit, it must then dry out and have a higher new source of heat to ignite it. For us that comes by repentance and asking the Father to give us His Spirit, or as Jim Cymbala says, to ask for a fresh wind and a fresh fire.

*"If you then, though you are evil,
know how to give good gifts to your children,
how much more will your Father in heaven
give the Holy Spirit to those who ask him!"*
LUKE 11:13

Fan into Flame

I had thought by many of my parenting techniques that I was fanning into flame the gifts that God had within my children. But the fan God speaks of is a gentle refreshing breeze, softly blowing and caressing that tiny flame. Many times I operated more on the hurricane level, which will either extinguish that flame or create a wildfire.

For this reason I remind you to fan into flame the gift of God,
which is in you through the laying on of my hands.
2 TIMOTHY 1:6

I believe that this verse referring to the laying on of my hands implies several things in how we are to fan into flame another person's gift. One touching another is a way of intimacy, friendship, and close relationship. Also, the picture I have of this is that of walking beside another with my arm over their shoulders mentoring them, and leading the way, not driving them in front of me. I think my boys will testify that I did this type of parenting as well. One thing I have had to do is forgive myself for not being the perfect parent and asking my boys to do so also. Some would also say that the reference to "laying on of my hands" could mean discipline and that, too, is an important part of parenting. But, discipline does not just mean punishment; it means training.

As a coach, that was an important part of my job, to train my players in various skills that they needed to play the game well and also to develop endurance. Without both skill and endurance, they would have a greater chance of injury and certainly would not be successful in a game. Isn't that what we parents really want for our children, to participate in life with skill and endurance and to run their race well?

Therefore, since we are surrounded by such a great cloud of witnesses,
let us throw off everything that hinders and the sin that so easily entangles.
And let us run with perseverance the race marked out for us...
HEBREWS 12:1

I know that as a parent I did the best I knew how at the time, and wanted the best for my children. I am sure most parents do the same. Most of us need to forgive ourselves for not being a perfect parent, and our children just need to be grateful that we were good parents. For there has only been one perfect parent and look what a mess some of His children get themselves into, myself included.

Power

Most of us desire power for ourselves. We seek it in different ways. We know that money, political offices, corporate positions, popularity, beauty, sports, musical or acting talent all give us a certain amount of power over others. But when we desire power over other people, it implies a pushing down upon them. The picture is one of us standing on the backs of others. We are the king of the mountain. But the power that Jesus talks about is the polar opposite. It is a power that is on the bottom and lifts others up.

When the boys were little we were visiting a new neighbor. I was in the kitchen area talking with her and the boys went in the backyard to look at her pool. We were standing there watching them and my youngest, who was about four, jumped in the pool over his head. His older brother, who was six, immediately jumped in and picked him up holding him above the water. I ran to get them out and when I reached for my youngest son, there was his older brother holding him up and holding his own breath under the water. That is the kind of power that Jesus promises us.

Sitting down, Jesus called the Twelve and said,
"Anyone who wants to be first must be the very last,
and the servant of all."
MARK 9:35

Who then do you think has the most real power, the one who has scrambled his way to the top, or the one who is at the bottom holding everyone else up?

Greater love hath no man than this,
that a man lay down his life for his friends.
JOHN 15:13

I still see my oldest son's eyes today looking up at me from under the water as he held his brother up. But how many of us have that kind of sacrificial love for others? Are we truly willing to be last in order to lift others up? Are we willing to be on the bottom in order to save our brother? Jesus did far more than this, for He died even for His enemies.

Once you were alienated from God and were
enemies in your minds because of your evil behavior.
But now he has reconciled you by Christ's physical body
through death to present you holy in his sight,
without blemish and free from accusation…
COLOSSIANS 1:21–22

Work Out

There is a verse in the Bible that has created a lot of controversy and theological debate though the years between grace and works. Many people may feel that they are just not "good enough" for God while others believe their moral practices and works give them a special ticket into heaven. This verse is:

Therefore, my dear friends, as you have always obeyed—
not only in my presence,
but now much more in my absence—
continue to work out your salvation with fear and trembling…
PHILIPPIANS 2:12

Much of my career was spent as a coach. I believe that God did this far more to teach me than I ever taught my players. We had daily workouts or practice. In sports we work out for many reasons, such as to develop skills in particular areas, to develop endurance, and to build a team. I believe that is what God is telling us in this verse. I did not have my players work out in order to get on the team, but because they were already on the team! As a coach, I had to assess each of my players to determine their individual strengths and weaknesses and develop a work out plan for each of them and collectively as a team. This was not done as a punishment but to develop fully mature members of the team. That is what God wants each of us to do and be. Fully mature members of His team.

Have you not been showing up for practice and finding yourself sitting on the sideline? There is a position on God's team that can only be filled effectively by you. It is time to start working out and getting in the game.

God has given each of us a gift that needs to be put to use to build up the church. That is how we truly "work out" our salvation with fear and trembling or humility, not pride and arrogance.

There are different kinds of gifts, but the same Spirit.
1 CORINTHIANS 12:4

So it is with you. Since you are eager to have spiritual gifts,
try to excel in gifts that build up the church.
1 CORINTHIANS 14:12

"In the last days, God says, I will pour out my Spirit on all people.
Your sons and daughters will prophesy, your young men
will see visions, your old men will dream dreams."
ACTS 2:17

Refresh Others

Everyone who rides with me knows that I have a lot of stuff in my saddle-bags. It is a joke among us that if you have a need, ask Linda and she will check in the bag and most of the time pull out the needed item. But I have learned this through the years by not having something along that we needed. I cannot tell you how many horses I have helped by just carrying tubes of electrolytes with me. A horse can be stressed by overworking or by heat, especially early in the riding season when they are not fit and still have their winter coat and yet the days are warm. Electrolytes refresh them and supply much needed nutrients, sometimes even saving their lives.

A generous person will prosper; whoever refreshes others will be refreshed.
PROVERBS 11:25

This is how God tells us to relate to each other. We all will need times of refreshing and we can all be used at times to bring refreshing to others. There have been times when we have been riding and it was I who needed something and another of my riding companions had to reach into their saddlebag and pull out the needed item. I believe God wants us to need each other and to learn to live in relationship this way. Whenever Jesus met a person with a physical need He met that need first, then He addressed their spiritual need. I especially like the story of His meeting the woman at the well. In this story, it was Jesus with the physical need. He needed water. But the woman had no idea that by refreshing Jesus with water from the well she would be refreshed by the "living water."

Jesus answered her, "If you knew the gift of God
and who it is that asks you for a drink,
you would have asked him and he would
have given you living water."
JOHN 4:10

We can never out-give God. Look around today for someone who needs refreshing. It may be only a phone call, a visit, or a listening ear. You may think it is you doing the giving but you just may be surprised by the "living water" that you receive in return. May you be refreshed today by refreshing others!

Truly I tell you, anyone who gives you a cup of water in my name
because you belong to the Messiah will certainly not lose their reward.
MARK 9:41

The Crest

I am blessed to have friends who share their blessings with me. A few years back, a couple who has retired and bought a place in New Mexico near Ruidoso invited several of us to stay with them and ride in the area. Joe could not get off of work, so I went with another couple from Texas. This would be one of the best trips that I had ever taken. I drove by myself to my friend's in Texas and then went with them the rest of the way. Ours hosts were terrific and went above and beyond to ensure that we were comfortable and had a wonderful time. They planned different trails for us to ride each day and other special activities. But for me, the crowning highlight was riding up the mountain for the first time and coming upon the Crest Trail at the top and seeing the almost 360-degree vista. We rode along the Crest for several hours but I wanted to stay there and never come down. I understood more what the disciples must have felt when they went to the mountaintop with Jesus.

After six days Jesus took Peter, James and John with him and
led them up a high mountain, where they were all alone.
There he was transfigured before them.
His clothes became dazzling white,

whiter than anyone in the world could bleach them.
And there appeared before them Elijah and Moses,
who were talking with Jesus. Peter said to Jesus,
"Rabbi, it is good for us to be here.
Let us put up three shelters—one for you,
one for Moses and one for Elijah."

MARK 9:2–5

Peter wanted to stay on the top of that mountain also. We rode The Crest trail on two different days. I cannot explain how I felt then or the feeling that I have now that overwhelms me at times when I long to go back to the top of that mountain. Charles M. Russell has said, "You can see what man has made from the back of an automobile. But the best way to see what God has made is from the back of a horse." The unusual aspect of this trail is that it is wooded all the way up the mountain without even a glimpse of a view. We did not have a clue what awaited us at the top. Sometimes our life may seem like that and we may be struggling to climb a mountain without knowing what awaits us at the top. My friend asked me to write a poem about our experience. I told her to pray and we would see what God said. That night he gave me the words to write and share with others. I know now why the disciples could not stay on top of that mountain nor could I. My work has to be done where the people are and that is in the valley below. It was a long climb up that mountain but I am blessed to be able to now "ride the heights" with Him even when I am in the valley. Wherever you are in your life's journey, I encourage you to keep on climbing. The view is worth it, my friend.

NEW MEXICO

Land of enchantment, New Mexico they say,
Land of my dreams, the place I'd love to stay.
Perched upon the Crest, above All space and time,
The troubles of this life are easy left behind.
From Capitan to Nogal, the vista with no end.
The Creator shows His splendor without the aid of men.
Few there are who find it, fewer still will climb,
Above the crowds toward heaven, to have such peace of mind.
Words no longer needed, written by His hand,
Those who ride together become Eternal friends.
Bound by the enchantment God touched upon this place,
To reveal a bit of heaven and help us on our way.
I cannot stay upon the mountain, my work is far below.
To be the hand of God, so others to may know.
The Joy in His presence, The Glory He displays,
For All His children's blessing, beyond the length of days.
Renewed by His Spirit, back to work I'll go,
Praying to return one day to these mountains from below.
For one thing I have learned, the View is worth the climb!

By L. Grajewski

The Lord said, "Go out and stand on the mountain
in the presence of the Lord,
for the Lord is about to pass by."
1 KINGS 19:11

He who forms mountains, creates the wind,
and reveals His thoughts to man,
He who turns dawn to darkness, and treads
the high places of the earth—
the Lord God Almighty is His name.

AMOS 4:13

Be Prepared

We were almost down the mountain that second day when calamity struck. My friend was riding in front of me on the trail when the ground under her horse's back right foot gave way. The side of the trail was very loose shell rock and he scrambled trying to get his footing. During this, my friend fell and went tumbling down amid boulders and brush. The horse without her weight was finally able to get his footing and scramble back onto the trail but my friend was hurt and down the side of the mountain about twenty feet.

While my friend's husband went down to help her, my other friend and I took care of the horse. He had several deep wounds on his legs where the rocks had cut him. We got out our first aid supplies and started taking care of him. My friend had sustained injuries also and could not climb back up. I usually have a long rope in my pack but forgot to check before this trip and it was not there. I did not remember that my husband had taken my rope out to use and not returned it. But, it was my fault for not checking my supplies before my trip.

We tied our lead lines together however and made a long enough rope for her husband to put around our friend, and then with the two of us pulling and her husband holding and pushing her, we were able to get her back to the trail. She had broken bones, lacerations, and a sprained ankle. Her husband helped her get back to the trailhead and we led the other horses back.

Jesus told us a story to help us with this.

The Parable of the Ten Virgins

"At that time the kingdom of heaven will be like ten virgins who took their lamps and went out to meet the bridegroom. Five of them were foolish and five were wise. The foolish ones took their lamps but did not take any oil with them. The wise ones, however, took oil in jars along with their lamps. The bridegroom was a long time in coming, and they all became drowsy and fell asleep."
"Therefore keep watch, because you do not know the day or the hour."
MATTHEW 25:1–5, 13

If you are reading this book, you are seeking to be prepared for your journey and for your destiny of riding the heights with Jesus throughout eternity. Don't give up; keep reading, keep praying, and keep riding with other followers of Jesus Christ. The top of the mountain or the trailhead may be just around the next curve.

Choices

When we lived in Slidell, a new family moved into our cul-de-sac. The very next morning, the mother was knocking on my door, stressed and in need of a friend. They had just moved back to the states after almost eleven years living abroad. They had spent a number of years living in a part of Indonesia where they had no choices at the grocery store. There would be one kind of detergent, one kind of rice or any other food or household item. She was feeling very overwhelmed by the move, busyness of our community, and the large stores with so many choices and decisions. We had a cup of tea, shared, laughed, and started the journey of friendship.

The most amazing part of this though is how she made the decision to purchase that particular house. The more she looked with the realtor, the more confused she had become. Then that night before viewing what was to become her house, she knelt and prayed asking God to just hang a star over the house she and her husband were to purchase. The next day while viewing the house, she gasped for inlaid in the brick of the house was a star!

Those who are wise will shine like the brightness of the heavens, and those who lead many to righteousness, like the stars for ever and ever.
DANIEL 12:3

Our modern life is filled with more choices than ever in history. Does life happen by choice or by chance? Every decision that we make affects what happens afterward. Some decisions can have serious consequences for years to come, not only to ourselves but others. My friend made the right choice because she first chose to consult God. The Bible gives an example of Wise Men making the right choice.

...and asked, "Where is the one who has been born king of the Jews? We saw his star when it rose and have come to worship him."
MATTHEW 2:2

After they had heard the king, they went on their way, and the star they had seen when it rose went ahead of them until it stopped over the place where the child was. And having been warned in a dream not to go back to Herod, they returned to their country by another route.
MATTHEW 2:9, 12

We have the choice of following, worshipping, and listening to the One who made the stars today also. This journey of faith may be long, we may have to go through deserts, face the wrath of others, and take detours in life. In other words, when we make the choice to follow Jesus Christ, our life may not turn out exactly like we planned. But when we follow the One who made the stars, He will lead us home.

Free Will

"Oh, Aslan," said Lucy. "Will you tell us how to get into your
country from our world?"
"I shall be telling you all the time," said Aslan.
"But I will not tell you how long or short the way will be;
only that it lies across a river.
But do not fear that, for I am the great Bridge Builder."
—C.S. Lewis In The Chronicles Of Narnia

The sovereignty of God versus the free will of man has been a question debated by theologians and other people for centuries. I believe that God knows what we will choose but He still allows us to make that choice. I also have seen how He has chosen to sometimes make a blessing out of my messy wrong choices. I have not always consulted Him when I had a decision to make; I was and am a very strong willed individual. That stubbornness and strong will has, at times, gotten me into trouble and at other times, kept me out of trouble. But because of my personal predisposition to this, my road to humility and submission to God has been bumpy to say the least. The best example I have found to explain this is from the *Chronicles of Narnia* when Lucy asks,

"Will you promise not to—do anything to me, if I do come?"

"You would not have called to me unless I had been calling to you," said the Lion.

I saw myself in Lucy. Because of my strong self-will, I also wrongly thought it was I who was seeking Him. I also bought into wrong thinking.

Some of us had to memorize a poem in high school, "Invictus," by William Ernest Henley. One line says, "I am the master of my fate: I am the captain of my soul." In a way, this is true, for God gives each of us the free will to choose to be the captain of our soul or to surrender to a Sovereign God.

...encouraging, comforting and urging you to live lives worthy of God,
who calls you into his kingdom and glory.
1 THESSALONIANS 2:12

God is calling to you today just as He called me. What will your choice be? If you choose to follow Jesus Christ, I will not promise you health, wealth, prosperity, and an easy and safe road in this journey, but only a safe destination with the Right guide and traveling companion.

My friend, will you make the choice today to join me on this Great Adventure to ride with Jesus Christ now and throughout eternity?

Trails

"Do not go where the path may lead; go instead where
there is no path and leave a trail."
—Ralph Waldo Emerson

All of my life I have loved narrow trails that wind through the woods and mountains. When I moved to Tennessee, my next-door neighbor introduced me to an area close to our homes where we could ride. One day, we noticed that it seemed someone was making a trail. We discovered that a young girl had written a grant and gotten permission to make a designated trail on the wildlife management land where we were riding. Through a series of events by default I became the leader of a volunteer group that makes and maintains horse trails on different wildlife management areas. These trails have become very popular and hundreds of people ride them every year from many different states. When my friend and I started riding by ourselves and just finding our way around this first area, we never dreamed what would grow from that. I did not have a vision of doing something good for others; I was just riding. Sometimes that is the way God leads us when we have the courage to get off the wide road and leave a trail.

Whether we plan on it or not, we all leave a trail behind us in this life, some obvious some not so much, but God says in the end, all will be revealed.

The sins of some are obvious, reaching the place of judgment ahead of them; the sins of others trail behind them. In the same way, good deeds are obvious, and even those that are not obvious cannot remain hidden forever.
1 TIMOTHY 5:24–25

Getting off the wide road and making trails is not easy. It is hard work, messy, and has a lot of challenges. The wide road that is already in place does seem a lot easier. Everyone else is on it so we think it must be the right way. Getting off the wide road or out of the church pew takes a lot of courage, but the results are worth it when you look back and see the trail that follows you.

"Enter through the narrow gate. For wide is the gate and broad is the road that leads to destruction, and many enter through it."
MATTHEW 7:13

Journey

*"You can see what man has made from the back of an automobile.
But the best way to see what God has made is from the back of a horse."*
—Charles M. Russell

It took me a lot of years to start really enjoying my journey in this world, to overcome my perfectionist and legalistic attitudes, and to be able to appreciate and value myself and others just as God created us. To be healed from the wounds of the past and set free to really live. I pray that by sharing my journey, others will be set free and be able to tear down their high places of sacrifice a lot sooner than I did. I now feel like the line from a Dr. Seuss book, *Oh The Places You'll Go!* God has taken me to some amazing places and I have seen things that many people never do. I never dreamed when I was a young girl growing up on that farm, all that God had planned for me. His plans are always much bigger than ours. I wonder what my life would have been like if I had just played it safe. Oh I might not have had some of the pain, hard times, and struggles, but I would have also missed the views from the top of the mountains. I have now ridden those mountains in seven different states and know God has others for me to ride before my journey here is finished.

I don't know where you are in your journey, dear reader, but I want to encourage you right where you are. Maybe you can't ride a horse, maybe you cannot walk on trails, but I promise God can and will use you and help you to find joy in your journey. I know that what He has and is doing for me, He also desires to do for you. The biggest obstacle to this that any of us will face is ourselves. For we have to be willing to do what God wants us to do, be who God wants us to be, and go where God wants us to go.

Have you spent most of your time looking at what man has made and fearing what man can do to you? Perhaps like myself, you need to get to a different place where you can have a different view of your situation or circumstances.

"Have you journeyed to the springs of the sea
or walked in the recesses of the deep?"
JOB 38:16

Long ago God confronted Job with this question. Job, too, thought his journey was too difficult and meaningless. But what a trail Job left for us to follow.

Stuff

When my father died just a few weeks after my grandfather, we were left with a big job to do. One thing we had to do was clean out the barn. They had used it as a workshop and for vet care also, but neither was very good at organizing and both kept everything. I think I took about twelve loads of stuff in our truck to the dump or salvage yard. But at the end, half hidden in the dirt, I found a beautiful treasure, a small painted glass swan dish. Amazingly it was in perfect condition. How it got there and survived all the activity through the years is a mystery. I still have that treasure on display in my home. God showed me through this that He has hidden and protected treasures in our lives amid all the stuff and chaos.

I will give you hidden treasures, riches stored in secret places,
so that you may know that I am the LORD,
the God of Israel, who summons you by name.
ISAIAH 45:3

I did not find this treasure until I got rid of all the stuff that was hiding it. We have to do the same in our lives. What stuff are you holding onto? God wants to help you clean out and get rid of the things that are cluttering and overwhelming your life so that the hidden treasures can be revealed. Sometimes we need help to get started on this big of a project. I did not clean out the barn alone. My husband, brother, and sister-in-law helped. There are people waiting to help you also; you do not have to do life alone. All you have to do is have the courage and determination to seek them out and to be transparent in asking for help. Now I am not telling you to run and disclose everything to everyone. You need to have discernment in this. But seek out Godly support and counsel.

When we finished cleaning the barn, we were all tired and dirty but we had found treasure and made order out of chaos.

My goal is that they may be encouraged in heart and united
in love, so that they may have the full riches of complete
understanding, in order that they may know
the mystery of God, namely, Christ,
in whom are hidden all the treasures
of wisdom and knowledge.
COLOSSIANS 2:2–4

Salt

Have you ever thought about all the uses we have for salt? It adds flavor to our food, it is a preservative, has antiseptic and healing aspects for wounds, is a de-icier, used to soften hard water, will put out a grease fire, cleans up oven spills, kills poison ivy, tests for rotten eggs and repels fleas. Wow, no wonder God compares us to being "salt" in the world!

"You are the salt of the earth."
MATTHEW 5:13

"Salt is good, but if it loses its saltiness, how can you make it salty again?
Have salt among yourselves, and be at peace with each other."
MARK 9:50

When we are salt to our world, what does this mean? I think God is telling us a number of important things here. We are to add flavor to whatever we are a part of. In other words, the Christian life is not meant to be boring and bland. We are to preserve and protect each other and to act with healing and cleansing from the wounds caused by sin. As a de-icier and water softener, our own hearts are first to be softened toward others and then to find ways to help others whose hearts have grown cold and hard. We are to be the ones who put out the fires of conflict and help clean up messes. And pests will be both repelled and destroyed by our salt, no longer able to cause harm to the body of Christ. But salt also is an irritant and when applied to a wound can cause pain as it brings healing. So it must be used with caution and with a gentle sprinkle, for we all know how unpalatable food that is over-salted is nor can we drink salt-water and live for long without it making us ill.

Let your conversation be always full of grace, seasoned with salt,
so that you may know how to answer everyone.
COLOSSIANS 4:6

An old saying used to emphasize a person's worth or value is, "he or she is the salt of the earth." God wants to use us in our world this way. When we are submitted to Him, "the SALT SHAKER" will yield a well-seasoned life and world.

Living Water

I do not do well in heat. When the temps get above 90 and the humidity is high, I just wilt. One year in June, I was on a trail ride with a group of friends. The temps were in the 90s and when we came back into camp, I thought I was going to pass out. I got off my horse, turned on the water faucet, and stuck my head under the running water. A friend went and got me a bottle of cold water also. After a few minutes, I felt much better.

When we are going through a stressful situation or a fiery test, we can begin to wilt spiritually and emotionally. If that goes on long enough, it will also affect us physically. Here is when we desperately need the "living water" that Jesus promises to restore us.

"Whoever believes in me, as Scripture has said,
rivers of living water will flow from within them."
JOHN 7:38

Jesus answered her, "If you knew the gift of God and
who it is that asks you for a drink,
you would have asked him and he would have
given you living water."
JOHN 4:10

Sometimes we are not able to go to the living water and need a friend to bring that water to us like my friend did for me. God desires to use us in this way. We need to be prepared and looking for others who need a drink from the living water. But, maybe you are in a situation where you feel abandoned by everyone and your thirst is getting desperate. There is One who will not abandon you and no matter what situation you are, in if you call upon Him and ask, He will lead you to the springs for your refreshing and healing.

"For the Lamb at the center of the throne will be their shepherd;
'he will lead them to springs of living water.'
'And God will wipe away every tear from their eyes.'"
REVELATION 7:17

My friend brought me water because she knew I was in need. Sometimes people do not know we are hurting and need help. I had to admit I was in trouble for someone to help me. But the results were worth it.

Becoming Real

This book has been all about getting real with others and myself and facing the truth. I am not a "super" Christian, have not reached the state of holiness, and am far from perfect. But I am also not who I used to be. Getting real means that I accept the lessons I have learned but still seek to learn more. I am beginning to learn that I don't even know how much I don't know.

In one of my favorite books, *The Velveteen Rabbit*, the Rabbit and Skin Horse are talking about the process of becoming real:

"Does it hurt?" asked the Rabbit.

"Sometimes," said the Skin Horse, for he was always truthful. "When you are Real you don't mind being hurt."

"Does it happen all at once, like being wound up," he asked, "or bit by bit?"

"It doesn't happen all at once," said the Skin Horse. "You become. It takes a long time. That's why it doesn't happen often to people who break easily, or have sharp edges, or who have to be carefully kept. Generally, by the time you are Real, most of your hair has been loved off, and your eyes drop out and you get loose in your joints and very shabby. But these things don't matter at all, because once you are Real you can't be ugly, except to people who don't understand."

For some, it takes longer to get real than others. If we are bound up in our high places of perfectionism and people pleasing, it will be almost impossible. The peace I have received in exchange however is immeasurable.

Brothers and sisters, I do not consider myself
yet to have taken hold of it. But one thing I do:
Forgetting what is behind and straining toward what is ahead...
PHILIPPIANS 3:13

It may seem strange to many at a time in my life where I should be slowing down and winding down, God seems to be winding me up and sending me out. Maybe it is because I am finally becoming real.

Broken Cisterns

A cistern is designed to be a leak-proof receptacle to hold and store water. They are invaluable in areas where water is scarce. But if one is built poorly or damaged, it will no longer hold water; it is a broken cistern.

Our Nation and, in fact, our world is in a time of crises. Japan has just experienced the worst earthquake and tsunami in history, with thousands of deaths and massive devastation. There is a nuclear plant that is spewing radiation there also. But, the crisis here is no less threatening. According to statistics, 40 percent of all children are now born out of marriage to single mothers and there are over one million abortions each year. According to the US Bureau of Census, 29.9 percent of single mothers live in poverty. A Nation cannot be healthy and sustain itself this way. We have drug and alcohol abuse at epidemic rates. Yet according to SAMSHA, most adults with an alcohol or drug problem don't recognize that they need help. According to the National Institute of Mental Health 26.2 percent of adults eighteen and older suffer from a diagnosable mental illness in any given year. We are trying to drink from our broken cisterns and this nation is ill because of it.

"My people have committed two sins:
They have forsaken me, the spring of living water,

and have dug their own cisterns,
broken cisterns that cannot hold water."
JEREMIAH 2:13

My precious reader, you may be crying out today for help or you may not recognize your own need and instead be blaming someone else. I have been there, but there is a healing balm and there is living water. I believe that God desires to heal and restore this Nation. Not to the place that it was; that only brought us to this point. But to the place He created and desires us to be. There is a line from a poem by William Ross Wallace, "the hand that rocks the cradle rules the world." I am crying out to the women of this Nation and World to turn from their broken cisterns and come drink from the "living water" that you and your children might fully live.

I will give them a heart to know me,
that I am the LORD. They will be my people,
and I will be their God, for they will return
to me with all their heart.
JEREMIAH 24:7

THE HAND THAT ROCKS THE CRADLE

William Ross Wallace (1819–1881)

Blessings on the hand of women!
Angels guard its strength and grace,
In the palace, cottage, hovel,
Oh, no matter where the place;
Would that never storms assailed it,
Rainbows ever gently curled;
For the hand that rocks the cradle
Is the hand that rules the world.
Infancy's the tender fountain,
Power may with beauty flow,
Mother's first to guide the streamlets,
From them souls unresting grow—
Grow on for the good or evil,
Sunshine streamed or evil hurled;
For the hand that rocks the cradle
Is the hand that rules the world.
Woman, how divine your mission
Here upon our natal sod!
Keep, oh, keep the young heart open
Always to the breath of God!
All true trophies of the ages
Are from mother-love impearled;
For the hand that rocks the cradle
Is the hand that rules the world.
Blessings on the hand of women!
Fathers, sons, and daughters cry,
And the sacred song is mingled
With the worship in the sky—
Mingles where no tempest darkens,

Rainbows evermore are hurled;
For the hand that rocks the cradle
Is the hand that rules the world.

Trees

I have loved trees all of my life. As a child, I would climb them and sit on the limbs looking out over the yard or countryside. I would dream as I played in them or under their shade. Trees are an integral and enriching part of all of our lives. They provide shelter, food, oxygen, and beauty. One year we took the boys on vacation to visit the Redwood forests in California. The magnificence of those trees and the centuries they have stood is awe-inspiring. Yet our Creator says that is what He wants to do with each of us.

...and provide for those who grieve in Zion—to bestow on them a crown of beauty instead of ashes, the oil of joy instead of mourning, and a garment of praise instead of a spirit of despair. They will be called oaks of righteousness, a planting of the LORD for the display of his splendor.
ISAIAH 61:3

There are some really important things to see in this verse. First there was suffering, grief, and despair. We all live in a very difficult and broken world. There is evil and there is suffering. The second important thing to notice is that our planting and healing is the Lord's work and to show His splendor, not our own. The third thing to know is that out of our ashes, He can make great joy and beauty. In our humble position and out of our humiliation, He desires to raise us up and crown us with His beauty and glory. We can then provide shelter, the bread of life, the breath of life, and beauty to others in our world. This is not for our glory and not our work but God's.

When we were in the midst of our son's illness and we did not know if he would survive, I sat in the middle of those ashes in despair. But I also cried out to God for help and healing, not just for our comfort and blessing but so that we could give God the glory and share this hope with others. But, maybe you are raging at me and saying, "My son did not survive." Then even more, my precious one, God desires to give you the crown of beauty and joy instead of ashes. Even when I did not know my son would have healing, I came to the place where I determined in my heart that I would surrender to God and His will. That I would not grieve as those who have no hope and that I would continue to let Christ live in and though me.

Though the fig tree does not bud and there are
no grapes on the vines, though the olive crop fails and
the fields produce no food, though there are no sheep
in the pen and no cattle in the stalls,
yet I will rejoice in the LORD, I will be joyful
in God my Savior.
HABAKKUK 3:17–18

Life Abundantly

If living the life of faith in God through His son Jesus Christ gave us health, wealth, beauty, and power, who in their right mind would not want this? But will you serve Him for nothing? Will you serve Him when the fig tree does not bud and there are no grapes, no crops, no sheep or cattle, and no fruit? Will you serve Him if He does not answer your prayer your way? I wrestled with this much like Jacob wrestled with the angel. I, like Jacob, walk with a limp, but He blessed me in and through the time of wrestling.

Do you also walk with a limp? Then don't let go until God blesses you and you take hold of all that God has for you!

When the man saw that he could not overpower him,
he touched the socket of Jacob's hip so that his hip
was wrenched as he wrestled with the man.
GENESIS 32:25

But Jacob replied, "I will not let you go unless you bless me."
GENESIS 32:26

What does the abundant life look like? Will you win the lottery? According to *Milwaukee Magazine* a surprising 30 percent end up broke and many fall into dept, divorce, and drunkenness. Maybe you want to be a star. Yet many of those we see in the headlines daily suffering from alcohol, drugs, mental illness, and divorce. God promises us that we can experience life abundantly right where we are because He will come and live with us.

This truly is LIFE ABUNDANTLY, not to have an abundance of stuff, but to have LIFE living in and through us daily and sharing that LIFE with others.

What agreement is there between the temple of God and idols?
For we are the temple of the living God. As God has said:
"I will live with them and walk among them,
and I will be their God, and they will be my people."
2 CORINTHIANS 6:16

No Whining Just Shining

I confess I am a whiner. But I do not whine as much as I used to. I only give myself a few minutes once in a while to whine and have a pity party. I found out anyway that most of the time, no one wants to come to my pity parties. I am reminded of what Joyce Myers says about complaining or whining, "Complain and remain, complain and remain. The children of Israel complained and they wandered in the desert for forty years."

When I read that years ago, it really hit home and I decided that I was tired of circling the same mountain and replaying the same old tired whiny tapes in my mind. When I started replacing those lies from Satan with God's truth, I started shinning!

"Arise, shine, for your light has come, and
the glory of the LORD rises upon you."
ISAIAH 60:1

In the same way, let your light shine before others,
that they may see your good deeds
and glorify your Father in heaven.
MATTHEW 5:16

For God, who said, "Let light shine out of darkness,"
made his light shine in our hearts to give us the light of the knowledge of
God's glory displayed in the face of Christ.
2 CORINTHIANS 4:6

Whoa, what was that? God said let light shine out of darkness. You mean right in the middle of whatever trial or mess I am in, I am supposed to shine? But you're saying, "I can't do that. I am hurting too much. I am depressed. I am angry…" You are right; you cannot and I cannot shine on our own. We do not have light. But He says He will make His Light shine in our hearts. Then and only then can we be a reflection of Him.

How do we do this? His Word tells us this also by the knowledge in the face of Christ. In other words, by spending time reading and meditating on His Word and then spending time alone with Him in prayer. The closer we get to Christ, the more His light shines in us and the more light we have to reflect out of the darkness we may have to be living in. The amazing thing about shining is the more we shine, the more we are polished up to reflect even more light. The dark will not dispel or quench the light, but the light will push back the dark.

Gaits to Heaven

Out of my darkness, God has birthed a work for me to do and share. I am speaking up and reaching out to others with the healing freeing power of the Gospel of Jesus Christ. If you catch the play of gaits versus gate then you know my main focus is on people in the horse community but I will share and go wherever God leads. In fact, I have several medical professionals who send people to me to mentor.

Another thing God is doing is opening up opportunities for me to speak and share at horse events and rides. I always start my talks with the disclaimer: "I am not a preacher, I am not a theologian, and I am not a medical professional. I am here to share what God has done and taught me in my life. I am here to share my story of hope and encouragement." I am also seeking to simplify my life so that I will have more time to ride, love, and share with others. It took me a lot of years to have the courage to do this but also for God to equip me.

The purpose of this ministry is to help people connect with God, with others, and with support resources. It is a Biblically based ministry but I also share information about medical and secular support resources that have good reputations and a history of success. When someone comes to me for information I always tell them: "If you had cancer would you not only get yourself on the prayer list but also go to the best oncologist that you could find?" The Christian community must get rid of the stigma and shame around mental illness and stop telling people it is only a spiritual problem. The spiritual aspect is an important component but it is not the only one.

King Nebuchadnezzar, To the nations and peoples of every language, who live in all the earth: May you prosper greatly! It is my pleasure to tell you about the miraculous signs and wonders that the Most High God has performed for me. How great are his signs, how mighty his wonders!
His kingdom is an eternal kingdom;
his dominion endures from generation to generation.
DANIEL 4:1–3

There is a verse in the Bible that says he who is forgiven much loves much. The same is true of us, for whom God has done so much and we cannot be silent but must share this with others. For my heart's desire, dear reader, is for you to prosper greatly!

Prosper Greatly

What does this really mean? I have already shared about money not always being the answer. According to Wikipedia, "Prosperity is the state of flourishing, thriving, success, or good fortune. Prosperity often encompasses wealth but also includes others factors which are independent of wealth to varying degrees, such as happiness and health."

In fact, economic notions of prosperity often compete or interact negatively with health, happiness, or spiritual notions of prosperity. King Nebuchadnezzar is a perfect example of this. He had all the wealth and power one could imagine or desire, but he could not stop or control what was going to happen to him.

Nebuchadnezzar did not have health, he did not have happiness, and he did not have a spiritual relationship with God. He was not prosperous any more, was he? But God was not finished with him.

I, Nebuchadnezzar, was at home in my palace, contented and prosperous.
Even as the words were on his lips, a voice came from heaven,
"This is what is decreed for you, King Nebuchadnezzar: Your royal authority
has been taken from you. You will be driven away from people and will live
with the wild animals; you will eat grass like the ox.
Seven times (years) will pass by for you until you acknowledge that the Most High
is sovereign over all kingdoms on earth and gives them to anyone he wishes."
DANIEL 4:4, 31–32

I, too, was prideful. God had to bring me to the place where I could and would totally submit to Him and recognize that I could do no good thing without Him, but that I can do ALL things through and with Him. Like Nebuchadnezzar, the natural result is to desire this prosperity for others. And once the King acknowledged this, what was the result?

At the end of that time, I, Nebuchadnezzar, raised my eyes toward heaven, and my sanity was restored. At the same time that my sanity was restored, my honor and splendor were returned to me for the glory of my kingdom. My advisers and nobles sought me out, and I was restored to my throne and became even greater than before. Then I praised the Most High; I honored and glorified him who lives forever. Now I, Nebuchadnezzar, praise and exalt and glorify the King of heaven, because everything he does is right and all his ways are just. And those who walk in pride he is able to humble.

DANIEL 4:34, 36–37

Not only was his sanity restored because he gave ALL the glory and honor to the only One who is truly worthy, but his honor and splendor was restored also—not to the place that it was before—he became even greater and others sought him out! And it is now my good pleasure to share these things with you. For what God has done for others, He longs to do for you.

*"Do not be afraid, little flock, for your
Father has been pleased to give you the kingdom."*

LUKE 12:32

Dear reader, this is also my prayer and blessing to you:

> *Beloved, I wish above all things that thou mayest*
> *prosper and be in health, even as thy soul prospereth...*
> 3 JOHN 1:2 (KJV)

Do-Bes-Go

I pray that you are not as stubborn as I am and it does not take you as many years to be willing and submit to God as it did for me. I also pray that you do not have to go through what Nebuchadnezzar did before you humble yourself and acknowledge the Most High God.

I am so grateful that God gave us His Word to teach us and encourage us and I am also grateful that He left examples of very imperfect people that He still found useful. Their stories give me great hope. Maybe He can use me also.

What about you? Are you now becoming ready to do what He wants you to do, be what He wants you to be, and go where He wants you to go? Or maybe you have been laughing and seeing yourself on the pages of my story but long ago you submitted. Then I thank you for finding my story worthy of your time. Pray for me dear reader, for the ministry He has given me, and for those He sends me to.

The people to whom I am sending you are
obstinate and stubborn. Say to them,
'This is what the Sovereign LORD says."
EZEKIEL 2:4

We who are people of the horse can be very obstinate, stubborn, and strong-willed. In fact, I have a friend who is a professional trainer and his motto is, "helping horses with their people." Pray for me as I seek to share and love them in gentleness. That out of my brokenness and the whole truth of my story they also may find the wholeness we all need through the WHOLE truth of Jesus Christ, who He is, and what He has done for us.

Then the woman, knowing what had happened to her,
came and fell at his feet and,
trembling with fear, told him the whole truth.
MARK 5:33

So the multitude marveled when they saw the mute speaking,
the maimed made whole, the lame walking, and the blind seeing;
and they glorified the God of Israel.
MATTHEW 15:31 (KJV)

Jesus did many other things as well. If every one of them were written down,
I suppose that even the whole world would not have room for the books that
would be written.
JOHN 21:25

The Three D's

My senior year of college, I was stressed, depressed, burned out, and ready to get out. I also made two D's. I felt like a failure. I did not get over that until years later when I made an incredible discovery in God's Word. When David had to run for his life and hide from King Saul, the men who ran with him were failures also. They were the three big D's: debtors, distressed, and discontent.

These failures were destined to become David's bodyguard and closest army, his "Mighty Men."

All those who were in distress or in debt or discontented
gathered around him, and he became their leader.
About four hundred men were with him.
1 SAMUEL 22:2

These were the chiefs of David's mighty men—they, together with all Israel,
gave his kingship strong support to extend it over the whole land, as the
LORD had promised...
1 CHRONICLES 11:10

How did these failures become David's "Mighty Men," listed this way in honor for us to remember throughout history? The process took twelve to fourteen years of fighting, running, and hiding in caves, until they became that "strong support" for the kingdom as the Lord had promised.

Just because you are in a time of adversity does not mean that you are not in the center of God's will and plan for your life. Just like these men, you also may need training and refinement that comes only this way. What promises from God have you given up on? Are you feeling like a failure? Hold fast to this lesson today and remember whom the world calls losers, debtors, distressed, and discontents, God calls His "Mighty Warriors" for the support of the Kingdom.

David summoned all the officials of Israel to assemble at Jerusalem: the officers over the tribes, the commanders of the divisions in the service of the king, the commanders of thousands and commanders of hundreds, and the officials in charge of all the property and livestock belonging to the king and his sons, together with the palace officials, the mighty men and all the brave warriors.

1 CHRONICLES 28:1

These were the people David gathered together to help his son Solomon build God's Temple. Likewise, you are not a failure; you have a destiny to fulfill. You and I are destined to be mighty men and brave warriors for His Kingdom!

Angels on Assignment

Whenever my boys went anywhere when they were young I would tell them, remember who you are and whom you belong to. How about you, my precious reader, do you know who you are and whom you belong to?

I have a friend who loves to say that sometimes God sends us friends who are really, angels on assignment. God Himself has said that we are only "a little lower than the angels."

Psalm 8:4-5: "what is mankind that you are mindful of them, human beings that you care for them? You have made them a little lower than the angels and crowned them with glory and honor."

The world and science will tell you that you are an accident of nature. You are just another animal in the animal kingdom. But I am telling you that you are a wonderful creation of God and that He has made you to be next in authority to the angels in His Kingdom, and He wants to crown you with glory and honor. Jesus took on this position when He left heaven for us. He took a demotion so that we could all be promoted into eternity.

But we do see Jesus, who was made lower than the angels for a little while,
now crowned with glory and honor because he suffered death, so that by the
grace of God he might taste death for everyone.
HEBREWS 2:9

Can you imagine what it must have been like for Jesus who created the angels to now be in a position below them? When I think about His doing that for me and you, it is hard to get my mind and heart around. Would you do that for someone who mistreated you? In our materialist and power-crazy world, most people would not even do it for their own children. Are you ready to be an angel on assignment? There is a work that God has prepared that only you can do. Are you willing to be demoted so He can promote you for His Kingdom purposes? Others may think you are crazy and feel sorry for you, and like Jesus on that Friday night, they may think you are finished. But, promotion day is coming!

...if we endure, we will also reign with him.
2 TIMOTHY 2:12

Flame On

I confess I am a super hero fan. I grew up reading comic books and watching the cartoons and movies. We all have a part of us that would love to have super powers and be able to right injustice and give the bad guy his punishment. But what happens when the bad guy is the one with the power? We have seen the results of that also in the super villains. There is a real super villain and he has been at work a long time trying to destroy mankind. He is very good at being bad. From the Garden of Eden until this day, we see the results of his villainous work in our world. He is called the Father of lies, deceiver, and destroyer.

Thy pomp is brought down to the grave, and the noise of thy viols:
the worm is spread under thee, and the worms cover thee.
How art thou fallen from heaven, O Lucifer, son of the morning!
how art thou cut down to the ground, which didst weaken the nations!
For thou hast said in thine heart,
I will ascend into heaven, I will exalt my throne
above the stars of God:

I will sit also upon the mount of the congregation,
in the sides of the north...
ISAIAH 14:11–13 (KJV)

How do we fight a real super villain? With super power of course! The TRUTH!

But we have this treasure in jars of clay to show
that this all-surpassing power is from God
and not from us.
2 CORINTHIANS 4:7

Very truly I tell you, whoever believes in me will
do the works I have been doing,
and they will do even greater things than these,
because I am going to the Father.
JOHN 14:12

But thanks be to God! He gives us the victory
through our Lord Jesus Christ.
1 CORINTHIANS 15:57

They triumphed over him by the blood of the
Lamb and by the word of their testimony;

they did not love their lives so much as to shrink from death.
REVELATION 12:11

If you have made it this far on our journey together, you either know who you are in Christ or that knowledge is being birthed within you. Don't let fear and only a little faith keep you from being the "super hero" He created you to be. I call to you now, FLAME ON!

Bucket Committee

I remember this phrase from a youth minister at a revival when I was a teenager. He used this to say that whenever we became "on fire" for the things of God, there would be a "bucket committee" standing by ready to pour water on us and put it out.

Often the bucket committee will come from within our own church or friends. Some will shun and reject you. They may gossip about you and say unkind and untrue things. Remember the story of Peter getting out of the boat and walking on the water to Jesus? The others, out of fear, tried to stop him. There is a sure defense against the bucket committees of this world and it is found within the Word of God.

"Do it again," he said, and they did it again. Do it a third time," he ordered, and they did it the third time. The water ran down around the altar and even filled the trench. At the time of sacrifice, the prophet Elijah stepped forward and prayed: "LORD, the God of Abraham, Isaac and Israel, let it be known today that you are God in Israel and that I am your servant and have done all these things at your command. Answer me, LORD, answer me, so these people will know that you, LORD, are God, and that you are turning their hearts back again." Then the fire of the LORD fell and burned up the sacrifice, the wood, the stones and the soil, and also licked up the water in the trench.

1 KINGS 18:34–38

FIRE...when anyone screams this word they get attention. We call 911 and the trucks race to the fire, lights flashing and sirens blowing. The bucket committee is ready. The very word "fire" brings fear to our hearts because we associate it with loss and pain. But when the FIRE of God falls on us, it is not to consume us but to refine us and make us more useful. These altars were the "high places of sacrifice" that the people had built. Only the fire of the Lord can consume the water from the bucket committee and those altars of pride, fear, and self. But when we have this kind of courage, the hearts of others will return to their first love.

If it is burned up, the builder will suffer loss but yet will be saved—
even though only as one escaping through the flames.
1 CORINTHIANS 3:15

Anonymity

I did not want to write this book but have done so out of obedience and love. I much prefer anonymity and being a stealth follower of Jesus Christ. When I was a teenager, I even memorized a poem about this: "I'm Nobody! Who are You?" by Emily Dickinson. One part says, "How dreary to be somebody! How public like a frog. To tell your name the livelong day to an admiring bog!" I just wanted to quietly live my life and do a few good things for God along the way. I did not want to be made uncomfortable or for my faith in Christ to cost me too much. This book is part of that wrestling with God and my ultimate surrender to Him.

Many years later I learned what being a FROG really means: **Fully Rely On God!** That is the only way anyone in the public eye can survive the bucket committees and keep from being a boiling frog.

I have led a number of the Beth Moore Bible studies. In one we had a CD by Travis Cottrell with the song "Jesus the One and Only." One line in particular has often played over and over in my mind and heart, "blessed anonymity count my life but loss, Jesus the One and Only fall over me dear cross." I am in no way shape or form comparing myself to this awesome woman of God who long ago gave up her comfortable anonymity. But I am very grateful to the equipping that God provided me through her.

What is more, I consider everything a loss because of the surpassing worth of
knowing Christ Jesus my Lord, for whose sake I have lost all things.
I consider them garbage, that I may gain Christ...
PHILIPPIANS 3:8

I am sure that I will face many a bucket committee in the months and years ahead, but I am no longer afraid. He has torn down the last of my high places of sacrifice and the fire of His spirit has and still is consuming the dross in my life.

The Great Adventure

God is always surprising me and taking me places that I did not think of. When God started this ministry, a group of us prayed for several months first. I wanted to make very sure of God's guiding and direction and that I had Godly counsel from others. During this, my husband told me, "I am 100 percent for you doing this ministry. You are the only person I know who has such a varied background and the experience and education to do this. God has uniquely prepared and equipped you through the years." But I thought I would be going to trail riding camps, other horse-related events, and church groups sharing God's Word and what He has done for and taught me. In other words, I thought it would be comfortable, safe, and close to home. I am doing those things also, but He had a bigger plan in mind.

I was invited almost 4 years ago to go on my first mission trip to the Pine Ridge Reservation in South Dakota. This reservation faces some of the most challenging circumstances in our nation. The Lakota people have been isolated and marginalized for centuries. Because of the dire poverty and living conditions many face depression and hopelessness, resulting in a suicide rate of 150% of the national average.

This is now the start of my fourth year of going twice a year in the love of Jesus to serve these beautiful and worthy people. I now call many of them friend and partners in ministy. It is just so amazing that God would send me for the Lakota have called themselves for centuries, 'the people of the horse'. I have volunteer churches and individuals who come with me to help. We do Horse & Bible camps for the children, Women's Bible Studies, a Recovery program, assist with a jail ministry, small home repair and constuction projects and other local Lakota lead projects such as the Crazy Horse Memorial Ride for Veterans. Our desire is to look where God is working, join-up and support the efforts of those there at Pine Ridge. This year we have also been invited to come to the Cheyenne River Reservation also in South Dakota and I will be spending a couple of weeks there.

When I started going to Pine Ridge God clearly gave me a word from Him on what this ministry would be based: **2 Corinthians 5:18** "All **this is from God**, who reconciled us to himself through Christ and gave us the ministry of reconciliation". I am to be His Ambassador of love and reconciliation. So in obedience and love I leave Tennessee and travel over 1300 miles to South Dakota. I cannot believe that God has chosen me!

Gaits to Heaven is an all volunteer 501c3 ministry and your donations are tax deductible. Checks should be made payable to: Gaits to Heaven and sent to: 1794 Buck Daniels Rd. Culleoka, TN, 38451. You may also give through Paypal on our website: www.gaitstoheaven.org.

Ever wonder what's at the end of the ride? I know that heaven is at the end of my ride and it can be at the end of your ride, too. But we are not there yet and I hope you will continue to follow where God is leading me and allow me to share these adventures with you. I am so grateful that He has called and enabled me to Ride the Heights with Him!

Dedication

This book is dedicated to my husband Joe who has been my strongest and most faithful supporter through the years. He has been and still is truly the "wind beneath my wings" and I know he always has my back. Without his support and encouragement I could not do what God has called me to do. He is always willing to do the behind-the-scenes work that has to be done but that few know about.

I also dedicate this book to my Mother and thank her for taking me to church every time the doors were open. Because of her faithfulness, my heart and life opened to God's will and purpose.

Made in the USA
San Bernardino, CA
17 October 2013